Arduino and Raspberry Pi Best informative Projects for future enhancement

Copyright © Anbazhagan.k
All rights reserved 2019.

Best 10 Arduino Projects for future development

CONTENTS

Circuit - CC and CV mode

Acknowledgments

The writer might want to recognize the diligent work of the article group in assembling this book. He might likewise want to recognize the diligent work of the Raspberry Pi Foundation and the Arduino bunch for assembling items and networks that help to make the Internet Of Things increasingly open to the overall population. Yahoo for the democratization of innovation!

Introduction

The Internet of Things (IOT) is a perplexing idea comprised of numerous PCs and numerous correspondence ways. Some IOT gadgets are associated with the Internet and some are most certainly not. Some IOT gadgets structure swarms that convey among themselves. Some are intended for a solitary reason, while some are increasingly universally useful PCs. This book is intended to demonstrate to you the IOT from the back to front. By structure IOT gadgets, the per user will comprehend the essential ideas and will almost certainly develop utilizing the rudiments to make his or her very own IOT applications. These included ventures will tell the per user the best way to assemble their very own IOT ventures and to develop the models appeared. The significance of Computer Security in IOT gadgets is additionally talked about and different systems for protecting the IOT from unapproved clients or programmers. The most significant takeaway from this book is in structure the tasks yourself.

1.LORA WITH RASPBERRY PI – PEER TO PEER COMMUNICATION WITH ARDUINO

L oRa is getting progressively mainstream with the appearance of IoT, Connected Cars, M2M, Industry 4.0 and so forth. In view of its capacity to impart to long removes with exceptionally less control it is ideally utilized by originators to send/get information from a battery fueled Thing. We have just examined the essentials of LoRa and how to utilize LoRa with Arduino. In case the innovation is initially expected for a LoRa Node to speak with a LoRa entryway, there are numerous situations wherein a LoRa Node needs to speak with another LoRa Node to trade data over long separation.

Along these lines, in this instructional exercise we will figure out how to utilize a LoRa module SX1278 with Raspberry to speak with another SX1278 associated with a microcontroller like Arduino. This technique can prove to be useful at numerous spots since the Arduino could go about as a Server to get information from sensors and send it to Pi over a long separation through LoRa and after that the Pi going about as a Client can get these data and transfer it to the could since it approaches web. Sounds intriguing right? In this way, we should begin.

Materials Required

1. 433MHz LoRa recieving wire – 2Nos

2. Raspberry Pi 3

3. Arduino UNO-or other variant

4. SX1278 433MHz LoRa Module - 2 Nos

It is accepted that your Raspberry Pi is as of now flashed with a working framework and can interface with the web. If not, pursue the Getting started with Raspberry Pi instructional exercise before continuing. Here we are utilizing Rasbian Jessie introduced Raspberry Pi 3.

Cautioning: Always utilize your SX1278 LoRa module with 433 MHz recieving wires; else the module may get harmed.

Connecting Raspberry Pi with LoRa

Before we get into the product bundles, how about

we prepare the equipment. The SX1278 is a 16-stick Lora module that conveys utilizing SPI on 3.3V Logic. The Raspberry pi likewise works in 3.3V rationale level and furthermore has in-manufactured SPI port and 3.3V controller. So we can straightforwardly interface the LoRa module with the Raspberry Pi. The association table is demonstrated as follows

Raspberry Pi	Lora – SX1278 Module
3.3V	3.3V
Ground	Ground
GPIO 10	MOSI
GPIO 9	MISO
GPIO 11	SCK
GPIO 8	Nss / Enable
GPIO 4	DIO 0
GPIO 17	DIO 1
GPIO 18	DIO 2
GPIO 27	DIO 3
GPIO 22	RST

You can likewise utilize the circuit chart underneath

for reference. Note that the circuit chart was made utilizing the RFM9x module which is fundamentally the same as the SX1278 module, consequently appearance may contrast in the underneath picture.

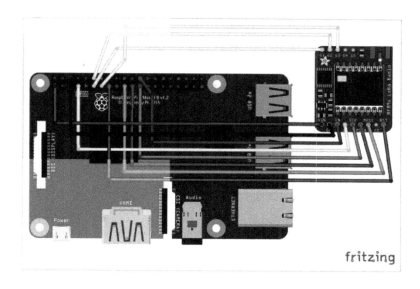

fritzing

The associations are quite straight forward, just issue you may face is that the SX1278 isn't breadboard good thus you need to utilize interfacing wires legitimately to make the associations or utilize two little breadboards as demonstrated as follows. Additionally few individuals recommend to control the LoRa module with independent 3.3V power rail as the Pi probably won't most likely source enough current. Anyway Lora being a low control module should take a shot at the 3.3V rail of Pi, I tried the equivalent and observed it to work with no issue. However, still take

11

it with a touch of salt. My association set-up of LoRa with Raspberry pi looks something like this underneath

Connecting Arduino with LoRa

The association for the Arduino module continues as before as that we utilized in our past instructional exercise. The main distinction will be as opposed to utilizing the library from Sandeep Mistry we will utilize the Rspreal library dependent on Radio head which we will talk about later in this venture. The circuit is give beneath

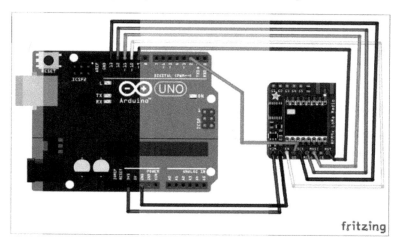

Again you can utilize the 3.3V stick on Arduino Uno or utilize a different 3.3V controller. In this task I have utilized the on-board voltage controller. The stick association table is offered underneath to assist you with making the associations effectively.

LoRa SX1278 Module	Arduino UNO Board
3.3V	3.3V
Gnd	Gnd
En/Nss	D10
G0/DIO0	D2
SCK	D13
MISO	D12

MOSI	D11
RST	D9

Since the module does not fit in a breadboard I have utilized the associating wires straightforwardly to make the associations. When the association are made Arduino LoRa arrangement will look something like this underneath

pyLoRa for Raspberry Pi

There are numerous python bundles that you can use with LoRa. Additionally generally the Raspberry Pi is utilized as a LoRaWAN to get information from various LoRa hubs. Be that as it may, in this undertaking our mean to do Peer to Peer correspondence between two Raspberry Pi modules or between a Raspberry Pi and an Arduino. Along these lines, I chose to utilize the pyLoRa bundle. It has a rpsreal LoRa Arduino and rpsreal LoRa Raspberry pi modules which can be utilized on the Arduino and the Raspberry Pi condition. Until further notice, we should concentrate on the Raspberry Pi condition.

Configuring the Raspberry Pi for LoRa module

As told before the LoRa module works with SPI correspondence, so we need to empower SPI on Pi and afterward introduce the pylora bundle. Pursue the underneath ventures to do likewise, subsequent to opening the terminal window of Pi. Once more, I am utilizing putty to interface with my Pi you can utilize your helpful technique.

Stage 1: Get into the arrangement window utilizing the accompanying direction. To get the underneath window

sudo raspi-config

Anbazhagan k

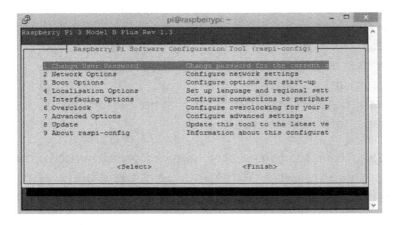

Stage 2: Navigate to interfacing alternatives and empower SPI as appeared in the picture beneath. We need to empower the SPI interface on the grounds that as we talked about the LCD and PI conveys through SPI convention

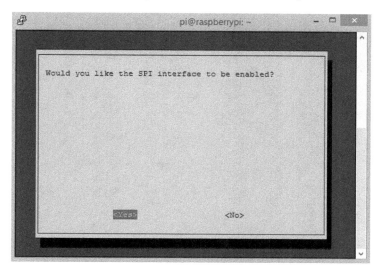

Stage 3: Save the progressions and return to the terminal window. Ensure pip and python is refreshed and afterward introduce the RPi.GPIO bundle utilizing the accompanying direction.

pip install RPi.GPIO

This bundle class will enable us to control the GPIO stick on the Pi. In case that effectively introduced your screen will resemble this

Stage 4: Similarly continue with introducing the spidev bundle utilizing the accompanying order. Spidev is a python official for Linux which can be utilized to perform SPI correspondence on Raspberry Pi.

pip install spidev

In the event that the establishment is effective the terminal should look something like this beneath.

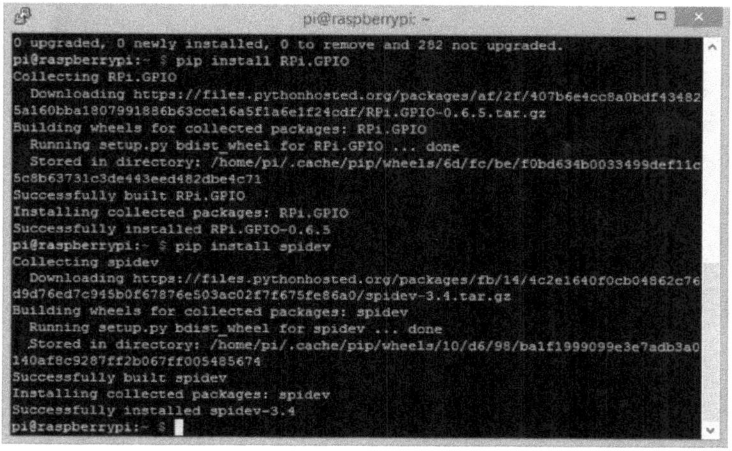

Stage 5: Next lets introduce the pyLoRa bundle utilizing the accompanying pip order. This bundle introduces the Radio models related with LoRa.

pip install pyLoRa

In the event that the establishment is effective you will see the accompanying screen.

The PyLoRa bundle likewise supports encoded correspondence which can be utilized with Arduino and Raspberry Pi consistently. This will improve the information security in your correspondence. In any case, you need to introduce separate bundle after this progression which I am not doing since encryption isn't in the extent of this instructional exercise. You can pursue the above github joins for more subtleties.

After, this progression you can add the bundle way data to pi and attempt with the python program given toward the end. Be that as it may, I was not ready to include the way effectively and henceforth needed to physically download library and utilize the equivalent straightforwardly for my projects. So I needed to continue with the accompanying advances

Stage 6: Download and introduce the python-rpi.gpio

bundle and spidev bundle utilizing the beneath order.

sudo apt-get install python-rpi.gpio python3-rpi.gpio

sudo apt-get install python-spidev python3-spidev

The terminal window should show something like this after both the establishments.

```
pi@raspberrypi: ~                                            _  □  ×
2 upgraded, 0 newly installed, 0 to remove and 280 not upgraded.
Need to get 47.1 kB of archives.
After this operation, 2,048 B of additional disk space will be used.
Get:1 http://archive.raspberrypi.org/debian stretch/main armhf python-rpi.gpio a
rmhf 0.6.5~stretch-1 [23.5 kB]
Get:2 http://archive.raspberrypi.org/debian stretch/main armhf python3-rpi.gpio
armhf 0.6.5~stretch-1 [23.6 kB]
Fetched 47.1 kB in 0s (54.0 kB/s)
Reading changelogs... Done
(Reading database ... 131597 files and directories currently installed.)
Preparing to unpack .../python-rpi.gpio_0.6.5~stretch-1_armhf.deb ...
Unpacking python-rpi.gpio (0.6.5~stretch-1) over (0.6.3~stretch-1) ...
Preparing to unpack .../python3-rpi.gpio_0.6.5~stretch-1_armhf.deb ...
Unpacking python3-rpi.gpio (0.6.5~stretch-1) over (0.6.3~stretch-1) ...
Setting up python3-rpi.gpio (0.6.5~stretch-1) ...
Setting up python-rpi.gpio (0.6.5~stretch-1) ...
pi@raspberrypi:~ $ sudo apt-get install python-spidev python3-spidev
Reading package lists... Done
Building dependency tree
Reading state information... Done
python-spidev is already the newest version (20170223-145721-1).
python3-spidev is already the newest version (20170223-145721-1).
0 upgraded, 0 newly installed, 0 to remove and 280 not upgraded.
pi@raspberrypi:~ $
```

Stage 7: Also introduce git and afterward use it to clone the python catalog for our Raspberry Pi. You can do that utilizing the accompanying directions.

sudo apt-get install git

sudo git clone https://github.com/rpsreal/pySX127x

When this progression is finished you should discover the SX127x sub registry in Raspberry Pi home organizer. This will have all the required records related with the library.

Programming Raspberry Pi for LoRa

In a distributed LoRa correspondence the module that is transmitting the data is known as a server and the module that gets the data is known as a customer. By and large the Arduino will be utilized in the field with a sensor to quantify information and the Pi will be utilized to get these information. Thus, I chose to utilize the Raspberry Pi as a customer and the Arduino as a server in this instructional exercise. The total Raspberry Pi customer program can be found at the base of this page. Here I will attempt to clarify the significant lines in the program.

Alert: Make sure the program record is in a similar catalog where the SX127x library envelope is available. You can duplicate this organizer and use it anyplace in case you wish to port the undertaking.

The program is really basic we need to set the LoRa module to work in 433Mhz and afterward tune in for approaching bundles. On the off chance that we get anything we straightforward print them on the reassure. As consistently we start the program by bringing in the required the python libraries.

```
from time import sleep

from SX127x.LoRa import *

from SX127x.board_config import BOARD

BOARD.setup()
```

For this situation the time bundle is utilized to make delays, the Lora bundle is utilized for LoRa correspondence and the board_config is utilized to set the load up and LoRa parameters. We additionally arrangement the board utilizing the BOARD.setup() work.

Next we make the python LoRa class with three definitions. Since we just indent to make the program fill in as a raspberry customer the class has just 3 capacities to be specific the init class, begin class and on_rx_ done class. The init class instates the LoRa module in 433MHz with 125kHz data transfer capacity as set in the set_pa_config strategy. At that point it additionally places the module in rest mode to spare power utilization.

```
# Medium Range Defaults after init are 434.0MHz,
Bw = 125 kHz, Cr = 4/5, Sf = 128chips/symbol, CRC
on 13 dBm

lora.set_pa_config(pa_select=1)

    def __init__(self, verbose=False):

        super(LoRaRcvCont, self).__init__(verbose)

        self.set_mode(MODE.SLEEP)

        self.set_dio_mapping([0] * 6)
```

The begin capacity is the place we design the module as recipient and get like RSSI (Receiving signal quality Indicator), status, working recurrence and so on. We set the module to work in ceaseless beneficiary mode (RXCONT) from rest mode and afterward utilize some time circle to peruse esteems like RSSI and modem status. We likewise flush the information in the sequential cradle onto the terminal.

```
def start(self):

    self.reset_ptr_rx()

    self.set_mode(MODE.RXCONT)

    while True:

        sleep(.5)

        rssi_value = self.get_rssi_value()

        status = self.get_modem_status()

        sys.stdout.flush()
```

At long last the on_rx_done capacity gets executed after the approaching bundle is perused. In this capacity the got qualities is moved into a variable called payload from the Rx cushion subsequent to setting the getting banner high. At that point the got qualities are decoded with utf-8 to print a client meaningful information on the shell. We likewise set the module back in rest mode till another worth is gotten.

```
def on_rx_done(self):
```

```
print("\nReceived: ")

self.clear_irq_flags(RxDone=1)

payload = self.read_payload(nocheck=True)

print(bytes(payload).decode("utf-
8",'ignore'))

self.set_mode(MODE.SLEEP)

self.reset_ptr_rx()

self.set_mode(MODE.RXCONT)
```

The rest of the piece of the program is simply to print the gotten qualities on the reassure and end the program utilizing a console interfere. We again set the board in rest mode even after end of the program to spare power.

```
try:

  lora.start()

except KeyboardInterrupt:

  sys.stdout.flush()
```

```
    print("")

    sys.stderr.write("KeyboardInterrupt\n")

finally:

    sys.stdout.flush()

    print("")

    lora.set_mode(MODE.SLEEP)

    BOARD.teardown()
```

Arduino Code for LoRa to communicate with Raspberry Pi

As I referenced before the rpsreal code bolsters both Arduino and Pi and consequently correspondence among Arduino and Pi is conceivable. It works dependent on the Radiohead Library from AirSpayce's. So you need to introduce the radio head library first to your Arduino IDE.

To do that visit the Github page and download the library in ZIP organizer. At that point place it in the library organizer of your Arduino IDE. Presently, restart the Arduino IDE and you will discover model records for Radio head library. Here we will program the Arduino to fill in as a LoRa server to send test bundles like 0 to 9. The Complete code to do the equivalent can be found at the base of this page as usual. Here, I will clarify couple of significant lines in the program.

We start the program by bringing in the SPI library (introduced of course) to utilize SPI convention and after that the RH_RF95 library from Radio head to perform LoRa correspondence. At that point we characterize to which stick of Arduino we have associated the Chip select (CS), Reset (RST) and Interrupt (INT) stick of the LoRa with Arduino. At long last we additionally characterize that the module should work in 434MHz Frequency and introduce the LoRa module.

```
#include <SPI.h> //Import SPI librarey

#include <RH_RF95.h> // RF95 from RadioHead Librarey

#define RFM95_CS 10 //CS if Lora connected to pin 10

#define RFM95_RST 9 //RST of Lora connected to pin 9

#define RFM95_INT 2 //INT of Lora connected to pin 2

// Change to 434.0 or other frequency, must match
```

```
RX's freq!

#define RF95_FREQ 434.0

// Singleton instance of the radio driver

RH_RF95 rf95(RFM95_CS, RFM95_INT);
```

Inside the arrangement work we will reset the LoRa module by dismantling its reset stick to low for 10 milli second to begin new. At that point we introduce it with the module that we made before utilizing Radio head library. At that point, we set the recurrence and transmission control for the LoRa server. Higher the transmission more separation your bundles will travel yet will expend more power.

```
void setup()

{

//Initialize Serial Monitor

  Serial.begin(9600);

// Reset LoRa Module

  pinMode(RFM95_RST, OUTPUT);
```

```
digitalWrite(RFM95_RST, LOW);

delay(10);

digitalWrite(RFM95_RST, HIGH);

delay(10);

//Initialize LoRa Module

while (!rf95.init()) {

  Serial.println("LoRa radio init failed");

  while (1);

}

//Set the default frequency 434.0MHz

if (!rf95.setFrequency(RF95_FREQ)) {

  Serial.println("setFrequency failed");

  while (1);

}

rf95.setTxPower(18); //Transmission power of
the Lora Module
```

```
}
```

Inside the vast circle work, we essentially need to send the information bundle through the LoRa module. This information can be in any way similar to sensor estimation of client order. In any case, for straightforwardness we will send roast worth 0 to 9 for each 1 second interim and after that introduce the incentive back to 0 subsequent to arriving at 9. Note that the qualities can be sent distinctly in a scorch exhibit position and the sort of information ought to be unit8_t that is 1 byte at once. The code to do the equivalent is demonstrated as follows

```
void loop()

{

  Serial.print("Send: ");

  char radiopacket[1] = char(value)};

  rf95.send((uint8_t *)radiopacket, 1);

  delay(1000);

  value++;

  if (value > '9')
```

```
value = 48;

}
```

Testing LoRa Communication between Raspberry Pi and Arduino

Presently, that we got both our equipment and program prepared we just need to transfer the Arduino code to the UNO board and the python sketch ought to be propelled on pi. My test set-up with both the equipment associated, looks something like this beneath

When the python customer sketch is propelled on

the Pi (utilize just python 3), if everything is working appropriately you must see the Arduino parcels got in pi however the shell window. You should see "Got: 0" to 9 like appeared in the picture underneath.

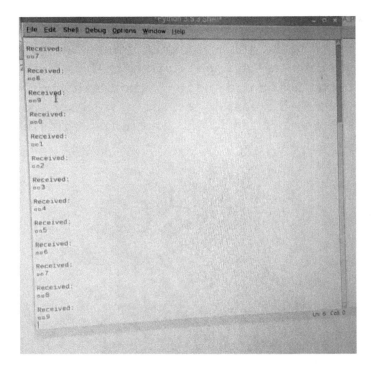

The total Raspberry pi code with all the required libraries can be downloaded from here.

You would now be able to move the Arduino server and check the scope of the module; it is additionally conceivable to show the RSSI esteem on the shell whenever required. Presently, that we realize how to set up long separation low control LoRa correspondence among Arduino as well as Raspberry pi we can continue with including sensor Arduino side and cloud stage on Pi side to make a total IoT bundle.

Expectation you comprehended the task and appreciated structure it.

Code

Lora Receiver Code for Raspberry Pi: (Download the required libraries from here)

```
from time import sleep
from SX127x.LoRa import *
from SX127x.board_config import BOARD
BOARD.setup()
class LoRaRcvCont(LoRa):
  def __init__(self, verbose=False):
    super(LoRaRcvCont, self).__init__(verbose)
    self.set_mode(MODE.SLEEP)
    self.set_dio_mapping([0]*6)
    def start(self):
    self.reset_ptr_rx()
    self.set_mode(MODE.RXCONT)
    while True:
      sleep(.5)
      rssi_value = self.get_rssi_value()
      status = self.get_modem_status()
      sys.stdout.flush()
```

```
    def on_rx_done(self):
    print("\nReceived: ")
    self.clear_irq_flags(RxDone=1)
    payload = self.read_payload(nocheck=True)
    print(bytes(payload).decode("utf-8",'ignore'))
    self.set_mode(MODE.SLEEP)
    self.reset_ptr_rx()
    self.set_mode(MODE.RXCONT)
lora = LoRaRcvCont(verbose=False)
lora.set_mode(MODE.STDBY)
# Medium Range Defaults after init are 434.0MHz, Bw
= 125 kHz, Cr = 4/5, Sf = 128chips/symbol, CRC on 13
dBm
lora.set_pa_config(pa_select=1)
try:
  lora.start()
except KeyboardInterrupt:
  sys.stdout.flush()
  print("")
  sys.stderr.write("KeyboardInterrupt\n")
finally:
  sys.stdout.flush()
  print("")
  lora.set_mode(MODE.SLEEP)
  BOARD.teardown()
```

Lora Server Code for Arduino:

```
//Arduino Raspberry Pi wireless Comunnication
through LoRa - SX1278
//Send 0 to 9 from Arduino through Radio head LoRa
without ACK
```

```
#include <SPI.h> //Import SPI librarey
#include <RH_RF95.h> // RF95 from RadioHead
Librarey
#define RFM95_CS 10 //CS if Lora connected to pin 10
#define RFM95_RST 9 //RST of Lora connected to pin
9
#define RFM95_INT 2 //INT of Lora connected to pin
2
// Change to 434.0 or other frequency, must match
RX's freq!
#define RF95_FREQ 434.0
// Singleton instance of the radio driver
RH_RF95 rf95(RFM95_CS, RFM95_INT);
void setup()
{


//Initialize Serial Monitor
 Serial.begin(9600);


// Reset LoRa Module
 pinMode(RFM95_RST, OUTPUT);
 digitalWrite(RFM95_RST, LOW);
 delay(10);
 digitalWrite(RFM95_RST, HIGH);
 delay(10);
//Initialize LoRa Module
 while (!rf95.init()) {
```

```
  Serial.println("LoRa radio init failed");
  while (1);
}

//Set the default frequency 434.0MHz
if (!rf95.setFrequency(RF95_FREQ)) {
  Serial.println("setFrequency failed");
  while (1);
}
  rf95.setTxPower(18); //Transmission power of the
Lora Module
}
char value = 48;
void loop()
{
 Serial.print("Send: ");
 char radiopacket[1] = char(value)};
 rf95.send((uint8_t *)radiopacket, 1);


  delay(1000);
 value++;
 if (value > '9')
 value = 48;
}
```

2.DIY LOCATION TRACKER USING GSM SIM800 AND ARDUINO

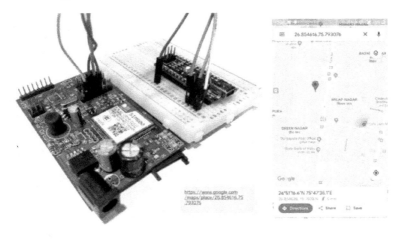

Self-driving autos and associated vehicles, is certain to change the manner in which we drive later on. Today organizations like Tesla are urging its proprietors to loan out their vehicles as robot taxis when not utilized, as of late its CEO Elon Musk took it to twitter to express it need more than 1 million robot taxis on street by 2020. This won't just effect general transportation yet in addition change the manner in which how coordinations work today.

With driver-less vehicles conveying travelers and Trucks conveying profitable freight, it gets the requirement for a Fleet Management framework wherein we have to follow them to know their area and guarantee in the event that they are at the perfect spot at the correct time. By and large a GPS

Module is utilized for any kind of area following yet here in this instructional exercise we will utilize GSM SIM800 module to assemble a straightforward Location following framework with Arduino. This GPRS following framework bargains the GSM modem and the microcontroller (Arduino) and is created on a PCB from PCBGOGO. It works so that when a telephone call is made to the GSM module, the module will check the area and sends it back as an instant message with Google guide connect to the number from which the telephone call is made. This connection when opened on telephone will stick the area of modem on Google Maps. Sounds Interesting enough!!? Along these lines, how about we begin.

Circuit Diagram

This GSM vehicle tracker framework will utilize GPRS of SIM800 GSM module which will be associated with a microcontroller like Arduino. Albeit both the GSM module and the Arduino sheets are accessible as isolated bundles I chose to make my own circuit consolidating them two on a solitary board to spare expense and space. The board can be controlled by a 12V connector or from the 12V battery in the vehicles/trucks, the on board buck converter will venture down the 12V to 4V for GSM module and as 3.3V for the microcontroller to work. The total circuit outline is given underneath.

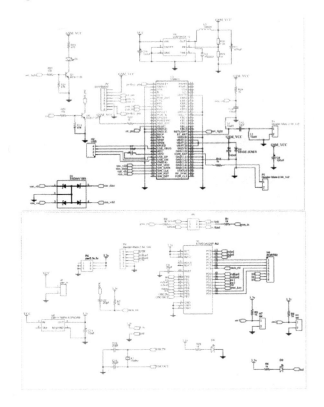

Further beneath I will part this circuit chart into squares and disclose them to ensure you can utilize them or change them as per your application needs.

LM2596 Power module

We have utilized the LM2596 Buck controller IC to give 4V to the SIM800 module from the info 12V. The SIM800 module requires around 2A crest ebb and flow when instated and looking for system, henceforth the power supply ought to have the option to

source that current, else the module will enter shut-
down mode, as well as consequently the LM2596 IC is
chosen which can supply upto 3A. The power supply
controller circuit is demonstrated as follows.

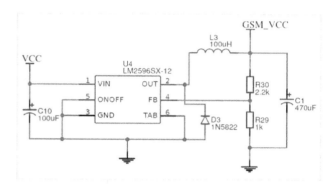

The 12V unregulated voltage is given to stick 1 and
the managed voltage is acquired on stick 2, which is
then gone through a LC channel of significant worth
100uH and 470uF separately to channel yield exchanging clamor. The yield voltage can be set by utilizing the resistors R30 and R29 framing the potential
divider circuit and associated with criticism stick as
appeared previously. The formulae to ascertain the
yield voltage for LM2596 is given beneath

Vout = 1.23 * ((R1+R2)/R1)

For our situation for the above graph, R29 is R1 and
R30 is R2. So I have chosen an estimation of 1k for

R29 as well as 2.2k for R30 to get a yield voltage of 4V. Note that the SIM800 module reacquires voltage among 3.7V to 4.2V to work typically.

Powering and Communicating with SIM800 IC

The SIM800 GSM modem is usually accessible as modem, yet we have utilized the exposed IC bundle to lessen board space and cost. Utilizing the SIM800 modem is practically straight forward, we just need to control the IC however the VBAT and GND sticks and after that utilization the PWR KEY stick to empower the modem by pulling the bind for 1 second. As a matter of course the stick is destroyed high inside to VBAT through a resistor.

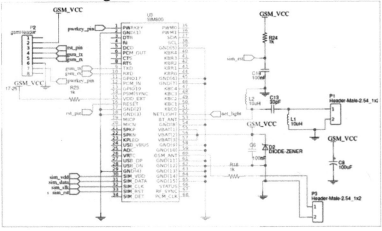

The voltage for VBAT originates from the controlled voltage (GSM_VCC) of LM2596 IC. The stick is named VBAT in light in case it is regularly control by a

Lithium Battery, so in case you are utilizing it on versatile gadgets, at that point you can avoid the LM2596 circuit and associate it straightforwardly to a lithium polymer battery. In that point we have the system pins associated with a 6-stick SIM card colder to interface with our SIM card. The NETLIGHT stick is associated with a LED, this LED will go about as a status LED to show the system status, however it is discretionary. So also the BT_ANT stick can be used to interface the module to a radio wire to discover organize association effectively, which is again discretionary.

At last we have the TxD and RxD pins destroyed out to a header stick, these two pins will be utilized to speak with a microcontroller like Arduino through the standard USART convention at 9600 baud rate. Different associations appeared in the circuit above is discretionary and does not hood any critical significance for this undertaking.

Microcontroller Side of GSM Locator

On the Microcontroller side we have the AT-MEGA328P chip structure AVR, which is the one utilized in Arduino UNO/Nano, yet here the controller is inserted legitimately on the board to speak with the SIM800 module. Since the SIM800 module works in 3.3V rationale, I chose to work the ATmega328 chip likewise with 3.3V itself since it additionally underpins both 3.3V and 5V working voltages.

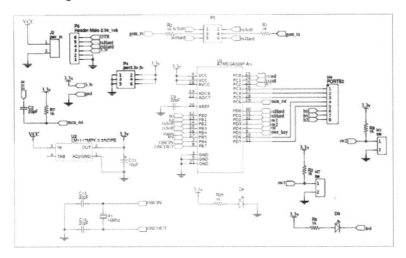

So as appeared above I have utilized the AMS1117 3.3V controller IC to direct 3.3V structure the information 12V and use it to control the Atmega328 IC. Despite the fact that the SIM800 chips away at 3.3V rationale level, it can likewise speak with Arduino Nano/Uno remotely without the need of any rationale level converters. The circuit additionally hauls out certain pins through headers to enable us to program the Atmega328 IC utilizing an outer FTDI software engineer like what we do with Arduino Pro smaller than expected in 3.3V mode.

Fabricating PCB for GSM Location Tracker

Since we has a circuit that joins the GSM module with a microcontroller we need to manufacture it on a PCB. Again to spare board space I chose to utilize a twofold side board with SMD parts, so I opened my

PCB planning programming and appointed the bundles and the segments utilized in above circuit and started structuring my PCB. When the Design was finished it looked something like this.

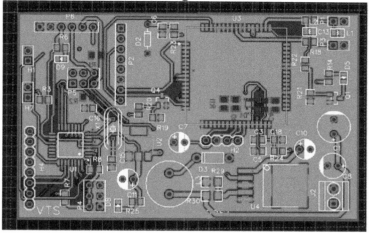

You can likewise download the structure records in GERBER position and create it to get your sheets. The Gerber record connection is given beneath

Download Gerber record for Arduino GSM Location tracker

Presently, that our Design is prepared the time has come to get them manufactured. To complete the PCB is very simple, essentially pursue the means underneath

Stage 1: Get into www.pcbgogo.com, join if this is your first time. At that point, in the PCB Prototype tab enter the components of your PCB, the quantity of layers and the quantity of PCB you require. Expecting the PCB is 80cm×80cm you can set the measurements as demonstrated as follows.

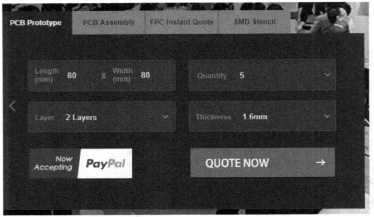

Stage 2: Proceed by tapping on the Quote Now catch. You will be taken to a page where to set couple of extra parameters whenever required like the material utilized track dividing and so forth. Yet, for the most part the default esteems will work fine. The main thing that we need to consider here is the cost and time. As should be obvious the Build Time is just 2-3 days and it just costs $5 for our PSB. You would then be able to choose a favored delivering technique dependent on your prerequisite.

Stage 3: The last advance is to transfer the Gerber record and continue with the installment. To ensure the procedure is smooth PCBGOGO checks if your Gerber record is legitimate before continuing with the installment. Thusly you can sure that your PCB is manufacture neighborly and will contact you as submitted.

Assembling the PCB

After the board was requested, it contacted me after certain days however dispatch in a conveniently named all around stuffed box and like consistently the nature of the PCB was wonderful. I turned on my patching pole and began gathering the Board. Since the Footprints, cushions, vias and silkscreen are flawlessly of the correct shape and size I had no issue amassing the board. For instance the SMD stack of my 68 stick SIM800 module were of extraordinary quality and looked impeccable like appeared underneath in the wake of patching the SIM800.

I continued with binding different segments and the load up was prepared in only a short ways from the hour of unloading the crate. Barely any photos of the board subsequent to fastening are demonstrated as follows.

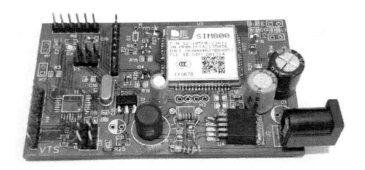

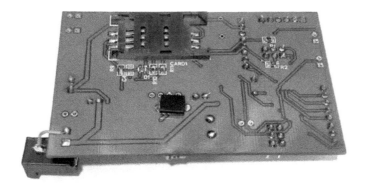

As should be obvious I have not utilized the micro-controller side of the board as it is still in testing stage, so for this instructional exercise I will attach the GSM module with an outer Arduino nano through the header pins. I will give an update once the micro-contrller part is likewise tried.

Connecting the Board to Arduino Nano

The outer header on the board marked as P2 can be associated with the Arduino Nano legitimately. Here I have associated the pins as per the table beneath

Arduino Nano	SIM800
Pin D12	PWR_KY
Pin D11	TxD
Pin D10	RxD
Gnd	GND

The power key associated with stick D12 is utilized to empower/debilitating the module after catalyst, this aides in sparing force when the module isn't utilized. Stick D11 and D12 is associated with Tx and Rx sticks individually, we will program the Arduino to utilized these pins as programming sequential to speak with the board. The set-up resembles this beneath once the associations are made.

Programming Arduino for GPRS Vehicle Tracking System

The total task can be part into three noteworthy segments, for example, accepting the call from the client, getting the GPS co-ordinates from SIM800, sending the GPS information to guest by means of SMS. Since we have as of now figured out how to send SMS utilizing GSM module as well as Arduino as well as handle calls with GSM module we won't examine much about that in this article.

Obtaining geo-coordinates locations (Latitude and Longitude) from SIM800 GSM module:

Acquiring GPS organize from GPS is simple contrasted with GSM. The accompanying AT directions will be utilized to get the area data in DD position from the SIM800 module

AT command	Description
AT+CGATT=1	Connect SIM to GPROS
AT+SAPBR=3,1,"CONTYPE","GPRS"	Activate bearer profile with connection type GPRS
AT+SAPBR=3,1,"APN","RCMNET"	Set VPN for bearer Profile
AT+SAPBR=1,1	Open Bearer profile
AT+SAPBR=2,1	Get the IP address of the bearer profile
AT+CIPGSMLOC=1,1	Request for

	location Pincode, latitude and longitude

Note: Make sure the SIM underpins 2G and GPRS plan before continuing with the above advances.

The directions when executed straightforwardly over sequential correspondence will react like this demonstrated as follows

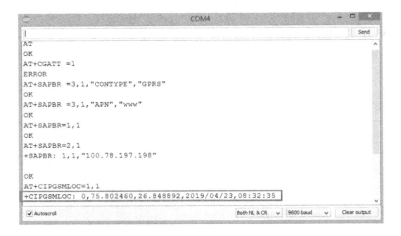

I have circled the last area result on the picture above. As should be obvious the reaction for the direction "AT+CIPGSMLOC=1,1" will be something like this

+CIPGSMLOC:
0,75.802460,26.848892,2019/04/23,08:32:35

Where 0 is the area Pin code (neglects to get in India), 26.8488832 is Latitude as well as 75.802460 is longitude. So we should trim these qualities out from this outcome and attach it to a Google Map connect to point the spot and address on a guide. The connection will be something like this

https://www.google.com/maps/
place/26.8488892,75.802460

We will utilize our Arduino code to do this and send the connection as a SMS to our telephone when mentioned.

The Arduino speaks with the SIM800 module however sequential correspondence with AT direction. For each AT direction we sent the module will answer character after character and if the outcome is effective the message will end with OK. In this way, before we begin with our program we compose a capacity called SIM800_send which will take in AT order as string and pass it to the GSM module utilizing SIM800. println order and afterward utilize the SIM800.read() capacity to recover the outcome from the SIM800 module and return it. The capacity is demonstrated as follows

String SIM800_send(String incoming) //Function to communicate with SIM800 module

```
{

    SIM800.println(incoming);  delay(100);  //Print
what is being sent to GSM module

    String result = "";

    while (SIM800.available()) //Wait for result

    {

    char letter = SIM800.read();

    result = result + String(letter); //combine char
to string to get result

    }

    return result; //return the result

}
```

Inside the arrangement work, we instate the sequential screen and SIM800 correspondence and 9600 baud rate and furthermore make the stick 12 (PWR_KY) low for 1 second to empower the GSM module. At that point we utilize the above made capacity to speak with the GSM module. We initially empower reverberation by utilizing "ATE1" and after that begin following the directions recorded above to get co-ordinates from GSM module. After each AT order we print the reaction on the sequential screen for troubleshooting reason, the code for the equivalent is given beneath

```
void setup() {

//PWRKY pin of GSM module has to be pulled low
for 1sec to enable the module

  pinMode(12,OUTPUT);

  digitalWrite(12, LOW);  //Pull-down

  delay(1000);

  digitalWrite(12, HIGH); //Release

  Serial.begin(9600); //Serial COM for debugging

  SIM800.begin(9600);  //Software serial called
SIM800 to speak with SIM800 Module

  delay(1000); //wait for serial COM to get ready

  responce = SIM800_send("ATE1"); //Enable Echo
if not enabled by default

  Serial.print      ("Responce:");      Serial.printl-
```

```
n(responce);

  delay(1000);

  responce = SIM800_send("AT+CGATT=1"); //Set
the SIM800 in GPRS mode

  Serial.print      ("Responce:");      Serial.printl-
n(responce);

  delay(1000);

  responce          =          SIM800_send("AT
+SAPBR=3,1,\"CONTYPE\",\"GPRS\"  "); //Acti-
vate Bearer profile

  Serial.print      ("Responce:");      Serial.printl-
n(responce);

  delay(1000);

  responce = SIM800_send("AT+SAPBR=3,1,\"APN
\",\"RCMNET\" "); //Set VPN options => 'RCMNET'
'www'

  Serial.print      ("Responce:");      Serial.printl-
n(responce);

  delay(2000);
```

```
responce = SIM800_send("AT+SAPBR=1,1"); //
Open bearer Profile

Serial.print        ("Responce:");        Serial.printl-
n(responce); //Open bearer Profile

delay(2000);

responce = SIM800_send("AT+SAPBR=2,1"); //
Get the IP address of the bearer profile

Serial.print        ("Responce:");        Serial.printl-
n(responce);

delay(1000);

}
```

Note that we have not utilized the last AT direction in the rundown which will really get the area co-ordinates. This is on the grounds that we will utilize them just when a call is put to the GSM module.

Inside the circle work, we check if the Module is stating anything. In the event that the module gets a get it will print out "RING". Thus, we make out program to check for RING purchase consolidating all the yield roast to string and contrast it straightforwardly with "RING". The code for the equivalent is demonstrated as follows.

```
if (SIM800.available()) { //Check if the SIM800
Module is telling anything

    char a = SIM800.read();

    Serial.write(a); //print what the module tells on
serial monitor

    incoming = incoming + String(a);

    if (a == 13) //check for new line

    incoming =""; //clear the string if new line is
detected

    incoming.trim(); //Remove /n or /r from the in-
comind data

    if (incoming=="RING") //If an incoming call
is detected the SIM800 module will say "RING"
check for it

    {
```

On the off chance that a RING is recognized, the time has come to bring the area information, trim the information and converter it to a google guide connection lastly send it as a SMS. In any case, before that we have to hang up the approaching call, to do this we utilize the direction "ATH". At that point we impair reverberation utilizing ATE0 and utilize the "AT +CIPGSMLOC=1,1" order to get the area information from the web.

```
Serial.println ("Sending sms"); delay(1000);

    responce = SIM800_send("ATH"); //Hand up the
incoming call using ATH

    delay (1000);

    responce = SIM800_send("ATE0"); //Disable
Echo

    delay (1000);

    responce = ""; Latitude=""; Longitude=""; //ini-
tialise all string to null

    SIM800.println("AT+CIPGSMLOC=1,1");    de-
lay(5000); //Request for location data
```

Once more, we utilize the equivalent while circle strategy to change over the yield characters to string. This time the string will have the reaction from the AT+CIPGSMLOC=1,1 direction which will contain the scope and longitude data as we talked about as of now. We will utilize the prepare_message() capacity to trim the estimation of scope and longitude. As should be obvious in the underneath test message

```
+CIPGSMLOC:
0,75.802460,26.848892,2019/04/23,08:32:35
```

The estimation of longitude is trailed by the main order and finishes with second direction. Likewise the estimation of scope begins with second order and finishes with third comma. We can utilize these attributes to get the scope and longitude esteems structure the program. Utilizing the beneath code

```
void prepare_message()

{

   //Sample Output for AT+CIPGSMLOC=1,1   ==>
+CIPGSMLOC:
0,75.802460,26.848892,2019/04/23,08:32:35  //
where 26.8488832 is Lattitude and 75.802460 is
longitute

   int first_comma = responce.indexOf(','); //Find
the position of 1st comma
```

```
int second_comma = responce.indexOf(',', first_comma+1); //Find the position of 2nd comma

int third_comma = responce.indexOf(',', second_comma+1); //Find the position of 3rd comma

for(int i=first_comma+1; i<second_comma; i++) //Values form 1st comma to 2nd comma is Longitude

    Longitude = Longitude + responce.charAt(i);

for(int i=second_comma+1; i<third_comma; i++) //Values form 2nd comma to 3rd comma is Latitude

    Latitude = Latitude + responce.charAt(i);
```

Since we have our scope and longitude esteem we simply need to join it to our Link with a comma in the middle of to frame the Link. The code for the equivalent is given beneath.

```
Serial.println(Latitude);        Serial.println(Longitude);

Link = Link + Latitude + "," + Longitude; //Update the Link with latitude and Logitude values
```

At last we can send the Link as SMS to a portable number. Here I have hardcoded the versatile number with the direction AT+CMGS="907923XXXX", ensure you supplant the order with your telephone number.

```
SIM800.println("AT+CMGF=1"); //Set the module
in SMS mode

    delay(1000);

    SIM800.println("AT+CMGS=\"907923XXXX
\""); //Send SMS to this number

    delay(1000);

    SIM800.println(Link); // we have send the
string in variable Link

    delay(1000);

    SIM800.println((char)26);// ASCII code of
CTRL+Z - used to terminate the text message

    delay(1000);
```

Testing the GPRS Tracking Device

Make the associations as examined and transfer the code to your Arduino Nano board. Addition the SIM card and ensure your system sign is set up. One approach to do this by checking the LED on your GSM module, which should streak once in at regular intervals. Presently open the sequential screen and you should see the accompanying messages in your screen

```
Responce:
OK

Responce:AT+CGATT=1
OK

Responce:AT+SAPBR=3,1,"CONTYPE","GPRS"
OK

Responce:AT+SAPBR=3,1,"APN","RCMNET"
OK

Responce:AT+SAPBR=1,1
Responce:
OK
AT+SAPBR=2,1
+SAPBR: 1,1,"100.94.39.103"

OK
```

This implies your GSM module is set for bringing coordinates and is prepared to accept approaching calls. You can basically call to your GSM SIM number from any number and you will see the call getting hanged up after initial couple of rings and you will get a message to number which you have entered in the program. The instant message will be contain the Google guide interface as demonstrated as follows

https://www.google.com
/maps/place/26.854616,75
.793076

Snap on the connection and you telephone will naturally take you to Google maps and plot the got area on your telephone with a red shading pin. You would then be able to explore to the area or get the location of that area. The above connection when opened seems this way

As should be obvious the blue dab is the area brought by my telephone's GPS and the red marker is the area given by our GSM module. True to form it isn't as precise as GPS however it would in any case work fine for our application and is extremely powerful since a similar module can be utilized to get calls and send SMS. In case you need to follow area utilizing GPS, at that point pursue the connection.

Expectation you loved the undertaking and delighted in structure it.

Code

/*Program to send Latitude and Logitute Information

from SIM800 to Phone via SMS on call request

```
 * Sample Output for AT+CIPGSMLOC=1,1   ==> +CI-
PGSMLOC:
0,75.802460,26.848892,2019/04/23,08:32:35      //
where 26.8488832 is Lattitude and 75.802460 is lon-
gitute
 * Link to send: https://www.google.com/maps/
place/26.8488892,75.802460  //where 26.8488832
is Lattitude and 75.802460 is longitute
 */
#include <SoftwareSerial.h> //Software Serial header
to communicate with GSM module
SoftwareSerial SIM800(10, 11); // RX, TX
String Link = "The current Location is https://
www.google.com/maps/place/"; //we will append
the Lattitude and longitude value later int the pro-
gram
String responce = "";
String Longitude = "";
String Latitude = "";
String SIM800_send(String incoming) //Function to
communicate with SIM800 module
{
    SIM800.println(incoming); delay(100); //Print
what is being sent to GSM module
  String result = "";
  while (SIM800.available()) //Wait for result
  {
  char letter = SIM800.read();
```

```
  result = result + String(letter); //combine char to
string to get result
  }


return result; //return the result
}
void setup() {
//PWRKY pin of GSM module has to be pulled low for
1 sec to enable the module
 pinMode(12,OUTPUT);
 digitalWrite(12, LOW);  //Pull-down
 delay(1000);
 digitalWrite(12, HIGH); //Release


 Serial.begin(9600); //Serial COM for debugging
   SIM800.begin(9600);  //Software serial called
SIM800 to speak with SIM800 Module
  delay(1000); //wait for serial COM to get ready
  responce = SIM800_send("ATE1"); //Enable Echo if
not enabled by default
 Serial.print ("Responce:"); Serial.println(responce);
 delay(1000);

  responce = SIM800_send("AT+CGATT=1"); //Set the
SIM800 in GPRS mode
 Serial.print ("Responce:"); Serial.println(responce);
 delay(1000);

 responce            =           SIM800_send("AT
+SAPBR=3,1,\"CONTYPE\",\"GPRS\"   ");   //Activate
```

Bearer profile

```
Serial.print ("Responce:"); Serial.println(responce);
delay(1000);
 responce = SIM800_send("AT+SAPBR=3,1,\"APN\",
\"RCMNET\" "); //Set VPN options => 'RCMNET' 'www'
Serial.print ("Responce:"); Serial.println(responce);
delay(2000);


 responce = SIM800_send("AT+SAPBR=1,1"); //Open
bearer Profile
        Serial.print    ("Responce:");    Serial.printl-
n(responce); //Open bearer Profile
delay(2000);
 responce = SIM800_send("AT+SAPBR=2,1"); //Get
the IP address of the bearer profile
Serial.print ("Responce:"); Serial.println(responce);
delay(1000);
}
void prepare_message()
{
//Sample Output for AT+CIPGSMLOC=1,1  ==> +CI-
PGSMLOC:
0,75.802460,26.848892,2019/04/23,08:32:35    //
where 26.8488832 is Lattitude and 75.802460 is lon-
gitute
 int first_comma = responce.indexOf(','); //Find the
position of 1st comma
  int second_comma = responce.indexOf(',', first_
comma+1); //Find the position of 2nd comma
```

```
  int third_comma = responce.indexOf(',', second_
comma+1); //Find the position of 3rd comma
  for(int i=first_comma+1; i<second_comma; i++) //
Values form 1st comma to 2nd comma is Longitude
  Longitude = Longitude + responce.charAt(i);
  for(int i=second_comma+1;i<third_comma;i++) //
Values form 2nd comma to 3rd comma is Latitude
  Latitude = Latitude + responce.charAt(i);
  Serial.println(Latitude); Serial.println(Longitude);
 Link = Link + Latitude + "," + Longitude; //Update the
Link with latitude and Logitude values
 Serial.println(Link);
}
String incoming = "";
void loop() {


  if (SIM800.available()) { //Check if the SIM800 Mod-
ule is telling anything
  char a = SIM800.read();
    Serial.write(a); //print what the module tells on
serial monitor
  incoming = incoming + String(a);
  if (a == 13) //check for new line
    incoming =""; //clear the string if new line is de-
tected
  incoming.trim(); //Remove /n or /r from the incom-
ind data
```

```
    if (incoming=="RING") //If an incoming call is de-
tected the SIM800 module will say "RING" check for it
    {
    Serial.println ("Sending sms"); delay(1000);
    responce = SIM800_send("ATH"); //Hand up the in-
coming call using ATH
    delay (1000);
    responce = SIM800_send("ATE0"); //Disable Echo
    delay (1000);
    responce = ""; Latitude=""; Longitude=""; //initial-
ise all string to null
        SIM800.println("AT+CIPGSMLOC=1,1");   de-
lay(5000); //Request for location data
    while (SIM800.available())
    {
    char letter = SIM800.read();
      responce = responce + String(letter); //Store the
location information in string responce
    }
        Serial.print("Result Obtained as:");     Ser-
ial.print(responce); Serial.println("********");
    prepare_message();    delay(1000);    //use   pre-
pare_message funtion to prepare the link with the ob-
tained LAT and LONG co-ordinates
    SIM800.println("AT+CMGF=1"); //Set the module
in SMS mode
    delay(1000);


    SIM800.println("AT+CMGS=\"9079259794\""); //
```

Send SMS to this number

```
  delay(1000);

    SIM800.println(Link); // we have send the string
in variable Link
  delay(1000);

    SIM800.println((char)26);// ASCII code of CTRL+Z
- used to terminate the text message
  delay(1000);
 }
 }


 if(Serial.available()) { //For debugging
 SIM800.write(Serial.read());
 }


 }
```

3.RS-485 MODBUS SERIAL COMMUNICATION USING ARDUINO UNO AS SLAVE

M odbus is a Serial Communication convention which was found by Modicon in 1979 and it is utilized for transmitting information over sequential lines between the mechanical electronic gadgets. RS-485 Modbus utilizes RS-485 for transmission lines. It ought to be noticed that Modbus is a product convention and not an equipment convention. It is separated into two sections, for example, Modbus Master and Modbus Slave. In RS-485 Modbus organize there is one Master as well as 127 Slaves each with novel location from 1 to 127.

Modbus is mostly utilized in PLCs (Programmable Logic Controllers). What's more, aside from this, the Modbus is additionally utilized in Healthcare, Transportation, Home Automation and so forth. Modbus has 255 capacity codes and there are for the most part three prevalent variants of Modbus:

- MODBUS RTU

- MODBUS ASCII

- MODBUS/TCP

What is the difference between Modbus ASCII and Modbus RTU?

Modbus RTU and Modbus ASCII talks a similar convention. The main contrast is that the bytes being transmitted over the wire are exhibited as double with RTU and as coherent ASCII with Modbus RTU. Modbus RTU is utilized in this instructional exercise.

This instructional exercise is tied in with utilizing RS-485 Modbus correspondence with Arduino UNO as Slave. Here we introduce Simply Modbus Master Software in PC and control two LEDs and Servo Motor by utilizing RS-485 as transmission line. These LEDs and servo engine are associated with Slave Arduino and constrained by sending esteems utilizing Master Modbus Software. Since this instructional exercise utilizes RS-485, it is prescribed to initially experience RS485 Serial Communication within Arduino Uno as well as Arduino Nano. RS485 can likewise be utilized with different controllers for sequential correspondence:

- RS-485 Serial Communication between Raspberry Pi and Arduino UNO

- Sequential Communication Between STM32F103C8 and Arduino UNO utilizing RS-485

We should start by investigating some foundation about the RS-485 and Modbus.

RS-485 Serial Communication

RS-485 is an offbeat sequential correspondence convention which doesn't not require clock. It utilizes a system called differential sign to move double information starting with one gadget then onto the next.

So what is this differential signal transfer method??

Differential sign strategy works by making a differential voltage by utilizing a positive and negative 5V. It gives a Half-Duplex correspondence when utilizing two wires and Full-Duplex requires 4 fours wires.

By using this method:

- RS-485 backings higher information move pace of 30Mbps greatest.

- It additionally gives greatest information move separation contrasted with RS-232 convention. It moves information up to 1200-meter most extreme.

- The primary bit of leeway of RS-485 over RS-232 is the numerous slave with single Master while RS-232 backings just single slave.

- Can have a limit of 32 gadgets associated with RS-485 convention.

- Another favorable position of the RS-485 is safe to the clamor as they utilize differential sign technique to move.

- RS-485 is quicker contrasted with I2C convention.

Connecting RS-485 with Arduino

RS-485 Module can be associated with any microcontroller having sequential port. For utilizing RS-485 module with microcontrollers, a module called 5V MAX485 TTL to RS485 which depends on Maxim MAX485 IC is required as it permits sequential correspondence over long separation of 1200 meters. It is bidirectional and half duplex and has information move pace of 2.5 Mbps. This module requires a voltage of 5V.

Pin-Out of RS-485:

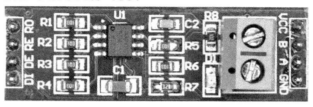

Pin Name	Pin Description
VCC	5 V
A	Non-inverting Receiver Input Non-Inverting Driver Output
B	Inverting Receiver Input Inverting Driver Output
GND	GND (0V)
RO	Receiver Out (RX pin)
RE	Receiver Output (LOW-Enable)
DE	Driver Output (HIGH-Enable)
DI	Driver Input (TX pin)

USB to RS-485 Converter Module

This is a USB to RS485 Converter Adapter module which supports WIN7, XP, Vista, Linux, Mac OS and gives a simple to utilize RS485 interface by methods for utilizing COM port in the PC. This module is fitting and-play gadget. There are no order structures, whatever is sent to the Virtual COM Port is consequently changed over to RS485 and the other way around. The module is totally self-fueled from the USB transport. In this way, no need of outside power supply for activity.

It appears as a Serial/COM port as well as is available from applications or hyper-terminal. This converter gives half-duplex RS-485 correspondence. The Baud rate range is 75 bps to 115200 bps, most extreme up to 6 Mbps.

To utilize this gadget there are different Modbus Software accessible in the web. In this instructional exercise a product called Simply Modbus Software is utilized.

Simply Modbus Master Software

Modbus Master Software application is expected to send information to slave Modbus RS-485 Arduino gadget by means of COM.

Essentially Modbus Master is an information correspondence test programming. You can download the Simply Modbus Master from the given connection and become familiar with it by alluding Software Manual.

Prior to utilizing the product, it is essential to get acquainted with the accompanying phrasings.

Slave ID:

Each slave in a system is alloted an extraordinary unit address from 1 to 127. At the point when the ace solicitations information, the main byte it sends is the Slave address. Along these lines each slave knows after the primary byte whether to overlook the message.

Function code:

The subsequent byte sent by the Master is the Function code. This number advises the slave which table to access and whether to peruse from or keep in touch with the table.

Supported Register Function codes:

Function Code	Action	Table Name
04 (04 hex)	Read	Analog Input Registers
03 (03 hex)	Read	Analog Output Holding Registers
06 (06 hex)	Write single	Analog Output Holding Register
16 (10 hex)	Write multiple	Analog Output Holding Registers

Supported Coil Function codes:

Function Code	Action	Table Name
02 (02 hex)	Read	Discrete Input Contacts
01 (01 hex)	Read	Discrete Output Coils
05 (05 hex)	Write single	Discrete Output Coil
15 (0F hex)	Write multiple	Discrete Output Coils

CRC:

CRC represents Cyclic Redundancy check. It is two bytes added to the part of the bargain message for blunder identification.

Tools Required

Hardware

- USB to RS-485 Converter Module
- Arduino UNO
- MAX-485 TTL to RS-485 Converter Module
- LED (2)
- 1k-Resistor (2)
- 16x2 LCD display
- 10k Potentiometer
- Servo Motor SG-90

Software

- Simply Modbus Master

Circuit Diagram

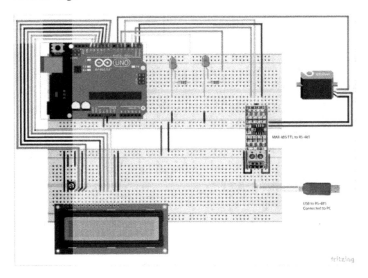

Circuit Connection between MAX-485 TTL to RS-485 converter module and Arduino UNO:

Arduino UNO	MAX-485 TTL to RS-485 Converter Module
0(RX)	RO
1(TX)	DI
4	DE & RE
+5V	VCC
GND	GND

Circuit Connection between MAX-485 TTL to RS-485 Module and USB to RS-485 converter:

MAX-485 TTL to RS-485 Converter Module	USB to RS-485 Module Connected with PC
A	A
B	B

Circuit Connections between Arduino UNO and 16x2 LCD display:

16x2 LCD	Arduino UNO
VSS	GND
VDD	+5V
V0	To control pin of potentiometer for contrast/brightness control of 16x2 LCD
RS	8
RW	GND
E	9
D4	10
D5	11
D6	12
D7	13
A	+5V
K	GND

Circuit Connection between 2 LEDs, Servo Motor and Arduino UNO:

Arduino UNO	LED1	LED2	Servo Motor
2	Anode through 1k resistor	-	-
5	-	Anode through 1k resistor	-
6	-	-	PWM pin (Orange)
+5V	-	-	+5V (RED)
GND	Cathode GND	Cathode GND	GND (Brown)

Programming Arduino UNO for RS-485 MODBUS Slave

The Arduino UNO is arranged as Modbus Slave. Additionally, Arduino UNO is connected with two leds as well as one servo engine so the slave arduino is controlled from the ace modbus programming. The correspondence between the Arduino UNO and the Modbus Master Software is practiced by utilizing the RS-485 module. For associating it with PC, the USB to RS-485 converter module is utilized. Furthermore, the Arduino UNO with MAX-485 TTL to RS-485 converter module, the entire arrangement will look record pursues:

For utilizing Modbus in Arduino UNO, a library <ModbusRtu.h> is utilized. This library is utilized for speaking with RS-485 Modbus Master or Slave by means of RTU convention. Install the Modbus RTU as well as include the library in the sketch by following Sketch->include library->Add .zip Library. Programming has some significant advances which will be clarified underneath.

At first, incorporate the required library. ModbusRTU library is for utilizing RS-485 Modbus correspondence, and the fluid gem library is for utilizing LCD with Arduino UNO, and the servo library is for utilizing Servo engine with Arduino UNO.

```
#include<ModbusRtu.h>

#include<LiquidCrystal.h>

#include <Servo.h>
```

Presently the LED anode sticks that are associated with Arduino pins 2 and 5 are characterized as LED1 and LED2.

```
#define led1 2

#define led2 5
```

Next the item for getting to Liquid Crystal class is pronounced with the LCD pins (RS, E, D4, D5, D6, D7) that are associated with Arduino UNO.

```
LiquidCrystal lcd(8,9,10,11,12,13);
```

At the point when LCD is done, Initialize servo item for class Servo. Likewise Initialize transport object for class Modbus.

```
Servo servo;

Modbus bus;
```

Next for putting away qualities for Modbus corres-pondence an exhibit is proclaimed with the three qualities instated with zero.

```
uint16_t modbus_array[] = {0,0,0};
```

In arrangement work, right off the bat the LCD is set in 16x2 mode and an appreciated message is shown and cleared.

```
lcd.begin(16,2);        //Lcd set in 16x2 mode

  lcd.print("RS-485 Modbus");    //Welcome Mes-
sage

  lcd.setCursor(0,1);

  lcd.print("Arduino Slave");

  delay(5000);

  lcd.clear();
```

After this, LED1 and LED2 pins are set as yield pins.

```
pinMode(led1,OUTPUT);

pinMode(led2,OUTPUT);
```

The servo heartbeat stick associated with PWM stick 6 of Arduino is joined.

```
servo.attach(6);
```

Presently for the Modbus correspondence the accompanying parameters are set. Initial '1' speaks to Slave ID, second '1' speaks to that it utilizes RS-485 to move information and '4' speaks to RS-485 DE&RE stick associated with Arduino UNO.

```
bus = Modbus(1,1,4);
```

The Modbus slave is set at 9600 baudrate.

The circle begins with the meaning of transport survey and bus.poll() is utilized to compose and get an incentive from the ace Modbus.

```
bus.poll(modbus_array,sizeof(modbus_array)/
```

```
sizeof(modbus_array[0]));
```

This technique is utilized to check if there is any information accessible at the sequential port.

In case there is any information accessible at sequential port the Modbus RTU library will check the message (check the gadget address, information length, and CRC) and play out the required activity.

For instance to compose or peruse any an incentive from ace, the ModbusRTU must get an unsigned 16-piece whole number exhibit and its length from the Master Modbus. This cluster conveys the information that is composed from the ace.

In this instructional exercise there are three exhibits for LED1, LED2 and Servo engine edge.

```
if (modbus_array[0] == 0)   //Depends upon value
in modubus_array[0] written by Mast

er Modbus

 {

   digitalWrite(led1,LOW);   //LED OFF if 0

   lcd.setCursor(0,0);
```

```
    lcd.print("L1:OFF");

  }

  else

  {

    digitalWrite(led1,HIGH);   //LED ON if value
other than 0

    lcd.setCursor(0,0);

    lcd.print("L1:ON");

  }
```

First to kill ON or the LED1 modbus_array[0] is utilized.

```
  if (modbus_array[1] == 0)   //Depends upon value
  in modbus_array[1] written by Master Modbus

    {

      digitalWrite(led2,LOW); //LED OFF if 0

      lcd.setCursor(8,0);
```

```
    lcd.print("L2:OFF");

  }

  else

  {

    digitalWrite(led2,HIGH);   //LED ON if value
other than 0

    lcd.setCursor(9,0);

    lcd.print("L2:ON");

}
```

Alongside turn ON or OFF the LED2 modbus_array[1] is utilized.

```
int pwm = modbus_array[2];

  servo.write(pwm);

  lcd.setCursor(0,1);

  lcd.print("Servo angle:");

  lcd.print(pwm);
```

```
delay(200);

lcd.clear();
```

Alongside set the edge of the Servo engine the mod-bus_array[2] utilized and worth is imprinted in the 16x2 LCD show.

Testing the Arduino UNO as Rs485 Modbus Slave

This completes the process of programming Arduino UNO for working it as MODBUS Slave. The following stage will test it as Modbus Slave.

After the circuit associations are finished and the code is transferred to the Arduino UNO, its opportunity to interface the USB to RS-485 module with the PC where the Simple Modbus Master programming is introduced.

Open the gadget chief and check the COM port as indicated by your PC where the USB to RS-485 Module is associated and after that open the Simply Modbus Master 8.1.1 programming.

1. After Simply Modbus Software is opened presently open the Write choice.

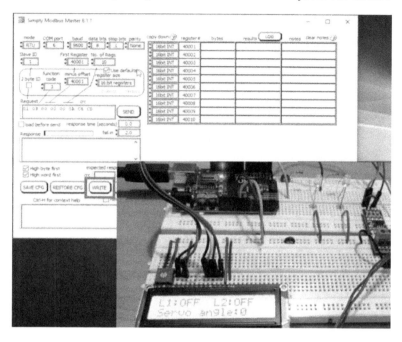

2. After the Simply Modbus Master Write is opened. Set the parameters

Mode in RTU, COM port as indicated by your PC (mine was COM6), Baud at 9600, Data Bits 8, Stop bit 1, Parity None as well as Slave ID as 1.

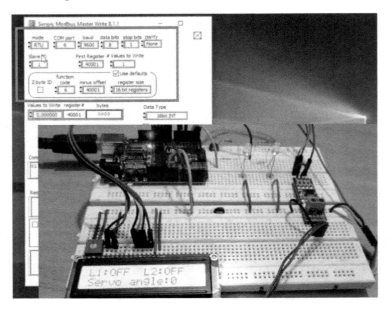

3. After that set first register as 40001 and qualities to compose is 3 and the capacity code as 16 (Write Holding Register).

After that compose 1 to 40001 (For LED1 on) and 1 to 40002 (For LED2 on) and 90 to 40003 (For Servo Motor Angle) and afterward snap SEND catch.

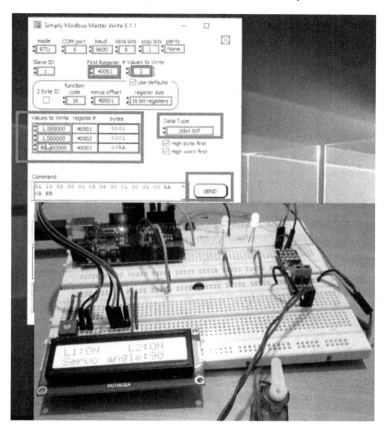

You can see both LED status is ON as well as servo edge at 90 degree.

4. After that enter 40001 as 1 as well as 40002 as 0 as well as 40003 as 180 as well as snap SEND catch.

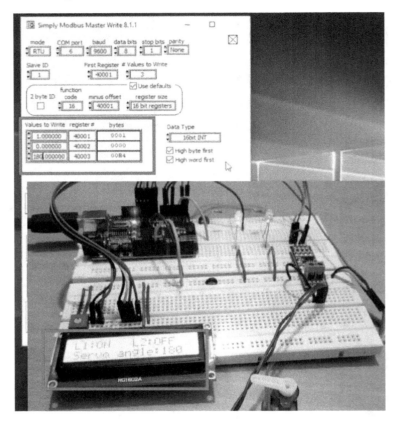

Presently Servo point at 180 and the led1 is ON and led2 is OFF.

5. Presently composing 135 to 40003 and 40001 as 0 and 40002 as 1.

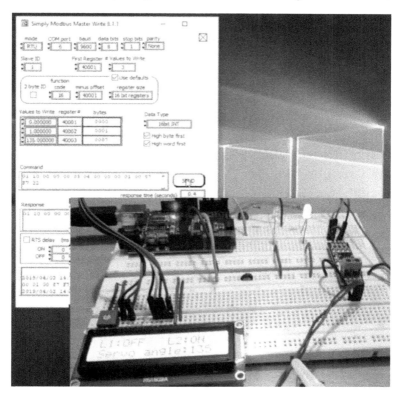

Presently the servo position is at 135 as well as led1 is OFF as well as led2 is ON.

This is the means by which RS-485 Modbus can be utilized in sequential correspondence with Arduino UNO as Slave. In next instructional exercise we will utilize the Arduino Uno as ace in MODBUS malediction.

Locate the total code is given underneath.

Code

//RS-485 Modbus Slave (Arduino UNO)

```
#include<ModbusRtu.h>      //Library for using Mod-
bus in Arduino
#include<LiquidCrystal.h>  //Library for using 16x2
LCD display
#include <Servo.h>         //Library for using Servo
Motor
#define led1 2      //Define as 2 led1
#define led2 5      //Define as 5 led2
LiquidCrystal lcd(8,9,10,11,12,13);   //initizlize lcd
object with pins (RS,E,D4,D5,D6,D7) for class liquid
crystal
Servo servo;            //Initilize servo object for class
Servo
Modbus bus;             //Define Object bus for class
modbus
uint16_t modbus_array[] = {0,0,0};   //Array initilized
with three 0 values

void setup()
{
 lcd.begin(16,2);       //Lcd set in 16x2 mode
 lcd.print("RS-485 Modbus");   //Welcome Message
 lcd.setCursor(0,1);
 lcd.print("Arduino Slave");
 delay(5000);
```

```
lcd.clear();


 pinMode(led1,OUTPUT);      //Led1 set as OUTPUT
 pinMode(led2,OUTPUT);      //Led2 set as OUTPUT
 servo.attach(6);        //Servo PWM pin 6
 bus = Modbus(1,1,4);     //Modbus slave ID as 1 and 1
connected via RS-485 and 4 connected to DE & RE pin
of RS-485 Module
 bus.begin(9600);          //Modbus slave baudrate at
9600
}
void loop()
{
     bus.poll(modbus_array,sizeof(modbus_array)/
sizeof(modbus_array[0]));      //Used to receive or
write value from Master


 if (modbus_array[0] == 0)  //Depends upon value in
modubus_array[0] written by Master Modbus
 {
 digitalWrite(led1,LOW);  //LED OFF if 0
 lcd.setCursor(0,0);
 lcd.print("L1:OFF");
 }
 else
 {
   digitalWrite(led1,HIGH); //LED ON if value other
than 0
 lcd.setCursor(0,0);
```

```
  lcd.print("L1:ON");
 }
 if (modbus_array[1] == 0)    //Depends upon value in
modbus_array[1] written by Master Modbus
 {
  digitalWrite(led2,LOW);  //LED OFF if 0
  lcd.setCursor(8,0);
  lcd.print("L2:OFF");
 }
 else
 {
   digitalWrite(led2,HIGH);  //LED ON if value other
than 0
  lcd.setCursor(9,0);
  lcd.print("L2:ON");
 }


  int pwm = modbus_array[2]; //Depends upon value
in modbus_array[1] written by Master Modbus


  servo.write(pwm);       //Write Received value (0 to
180) from Modbus Master
  lcd.setCursor(0,1);
  lcd.print("Servo angle:");
  lcd.print(pwm);            //Prints Angle in 16x2 LCD
display.
  delay(200);
  lcd.clear();
 }
```

4.INTERFACING VIBRATION SENSOR MODULE WITH ARDUINO

There are a some basic machines or costly types of gear which endure harms because of vibrations. In such a case, a vibration sensor is needed to see if the machine or hardware is creating vibrations or not. Distinguishing the article which is persistently vibrating is definitely not a dubious occupation if the best possible sensor is utilized to recognize the vibration. There are a few kinds of vibration sensors accessible in the market which can recognize the vibration bys detecting speeding up or speed and could give incredible outcome. Be that as it may, such sensors are too costly where the accelerometer is utilized. Accelerometer is delicate and can be utilized to make Earthquake finder circuit. Be that as it may, there are not many committed and modest sensors are likewise accessible to distinguish the vibrations just, one such vibration sensor is SW-420 which we are gonna to interface with Arduino Uno.

So in this undertaking, a fundamental vibration sensor module is interfaced with well known Arduino UNO and at whatever point the vibration sensor recognizes any vibration or snap a LED will begin flickering.

Vibration Sensor Module SW-420

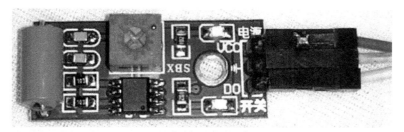

Vibration Sensor Module SW-420

This is a SW-420 vibration module, which can work from 3.3V to the 5V. The sensor utilizes LM393 comparator to distinguish the vibration over an edge point and give computerized information, Logic Low or Logic High, 0 or 1. During ordinary activity, the sensor gives Logic Low and when the vibration is distinguished, the sensor gives Logic High. There are three peripherals accessible in the module, two LEDs, one for the Power state and other for the sensor's yield. Also, a potentiometer is accessible which can be additionally used to control the limit purpose of the vibration. In this task, we will utilize 5V to power the module.

We utilized a similar sensor in Anti-Theft Alert System utilizing ATmega8 Microcontroller. Likewise a tilt sensor can be utilized to distinguish abrupt mishap.

Components Required

1. 5mm LED (Any Color)
2. Arduino UNO
3. USB Cable for Uploading Program
4. Jumper Wires(Hookup Wires)
5. SW-420 Vibration Sensor Module

Arduino Vibration Sensor Circuit Diagram

The schematic for interfacing Vibration sensor with Arduino uno is given beneath.

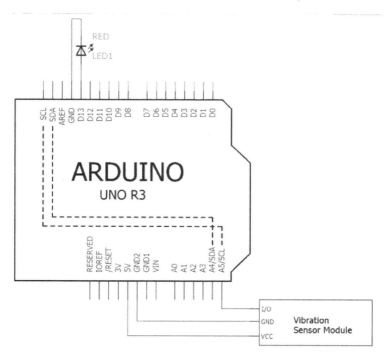

The LED is associated in the D13 stick. The module is controlled utilizing the accessible 5V stick in the Arduino. The Ground and the 5V stick are utilized to catalyst the Arduino though the A5 stick is utilized to get the information from the vibration sensor.

The circuit is developed where the SW-420 module and LED are associated with Arduino Uno.

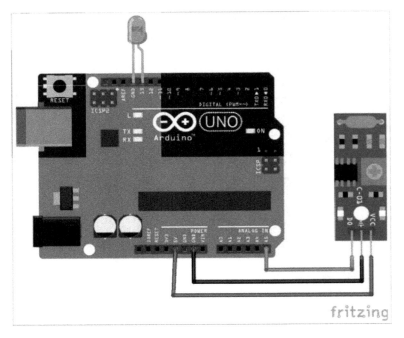

Arduino Uno Vibration Sensor Programming

Programming the Arduino UNO to interface vibration sensor doesn't require much exertion as just the info stick ought to be checked to make end. At first the Header Files are incorporated. The arduino header is incorporated since this instructional exercise was written in Eclipse IDE with Arduino expansion. This sketch will likewise work for Arduino IDE and keeping in mind that utilizing this sketch in Arduino IDE, there is no compelling reason to incorporate <Arduino.h> header.

```
#include <Arduino.h>
```

Here two macros are characterized for ON and OFF.

```
#define ON 1

#define OFF 0
```

The underneath proclamation is utilized for coordinating the LEDs and the Vibration Sensor. The vibration sensor is associated with stick A5. The inbuilt LED is additionally utilized which is legitimately associated in the board to stick 13. The 5mm LED is additionally associated with the stick 13.

```
/*

* Pin Description

*/

int vibration_Sensor = A5;

int LED = 13;
```

Two whole numbers are pronounced where the sensors present yield and past yield will be put away, which will additionally used to recognize whether the vibration is going on or not.

```
/*

* Programme flow Description

*/

int present_condition = 0;

int previous_condition = 0;
```

A similar stick which is pronounced as the fringe association, the course of the pins are arranged. The sensor stick as information and the LED stick as a yield.

```
/*

* Pin mode setup

*/

void setup() {

        pinMode(vibration_Sensor, INPUT);
```

```
        pinMode(LED, OUTPUT);

}
```

One capacity is composed to flicker the drove twice. The deferral can be designed by chaging the postpone esteem.

```
void led_blink(void) {

        digitalWrite(LED, ON);

        delay(250);

        digitalWrite(LED, OFF);

        delay(250);

        digitalWrite(LED, ON);

        delay(250);

        digitalWrite(LED, OFF);

        delay(250);

}
```

On top of it capacity, present and past condition is

looked at. On the off chance that these two are not same, the leds begin to squint until the both are same. In beginning, the two factors hold 0 and the drove stays off during the beginning of program. At the point when there is some virbraion, present_condition variable winds up 1 and drove begin to squint. What's more, again when vibrations stops both the vaiables winds up 0 and LED quits flickering.

```
void loop() {

        previous_condition = present_condition;

        present_condition = digitalRead(A5); //
Reading digital data from the A5 Pin of the Ar-
duino.

        if (previous_condition != present_condi-
tion) {

                led_blink();

        } else {

                digitalWrite(LED, OFF);

        }

}
```

This completes the programming the arduino UNO with Vibration sensor. The last advance will test the entire arrangement.

Testing the Arduino Vibration Sensor Circuit

The circuit doesn't require extra breadboard. It tends to be essentially tried utilizing the Arduino UNO Board. The drove is observed when the vibration sensor is hit or in case that it changes its state. The drove will flicker associated with Pin 13 of Arduino UNO when there is a few vibrations. In case the vibration sensor doesn't work, at that point please check the association and power. Maintain a strategic distance from any free association among sensor and microcontroller.

So this is the means by which a Vibration sensor can be interfaced with Arduino UNO.

Code

```
/*//
==========================================
==================================//
 * Vibration Sensor interfacing with Arduino
 */                                        //
==========================================
==================================//
#include <Arduino.h>
#include <stdio.h>
#define ON 1
#define OFF 0
/*
 * Pin Description
 */
int vibration_Sensor = A5;
int LED = 13;
/*
 * Programme flow Description
 */
int present_condition = 0;
int previous_condition = 0;
/*
 * Pin mode setup
 */
void setup() {
```

```
pinMode(vibration_Sensor, INPUT);
pinMode(LED, OUTPUT);
}
/*
 * Led blink
 */
void led_blink(void);
/*
 * main_loop
 */
void loop() {
previous_condition = present_condition;
present_condition = digitalRead(A5); // Reading digital data from the A5 Pin of the Arduino.
if(previous_condition != present_condition) {
led_blink();
} else {
digitalWrite(LED, OFF);
}
}
void led_blink(void) {
digitalWrite(LED, ON);
delay(250);
digitalWrite(LED, OFF);
delay(250);
digitalWrite(LED, ON);
delay(250);
digitalWrite(LED, OFF);
delay(250);
}
```

5.RS-485 SERIAL COMMUNICATION BETWEEN RASPBERRY PI AND ARDUINO UNO

Picking a correspondence convention for correspondence among microcontrollers and fringe gadgets is a significant piece of installed framework. It is significant on the grounds that the general execution of any installed application relies upon correspondence implies as it is identified with cost decrease, quicker information move, long separation inclusion and so forth.

Until now, we have seen RS485 Serial Communication between Arduino Uno and Arduino Nano, today in this we will see RS-485 correspondence between a Raspberry Pi and Arduino UNO.

RS485 Serial Communication Protocol

RS-485 is a nonconcurrent sequential correspondence convention which doesn't not require clock. It utilizes a system called differential sign to move twofold information starting with one gadget then the next.

So what is differential signal transfer method?

Differential sign strategy works by making a differential voltage by utilizing a positive and negative 5V. It gives a Half-Duplex correspondence when utilizing two wires and Full-Duplex requires 4 fours wires.

In this instructional exercise the edge of the servo engine associated with Arduino UNO is constrained by sending edge esteems from Raspberry Pi to Arduino UNO through RS-485 Serial correspondence. Raspberry Pi is utilized as Master and the Arduino UNO with servo engine is utilized as slave. Additionally it has a LCD 16x2 showcase to demonstrate the edge esteem that is gotten from Raspberry Pi.

Components Required

1. Raspberry Pi 3 B+ (With Raspbian OS installed)
2. Arduino UNO
3. MAX485 TTL to RS485 Converter Module (2)
4. SG-90 Servo Motor
5. 16x2 LCD
6. 10K Potentiometer
7. Bread Board
8. Connecting Wires

Pin-Out & Features of MAX-485 TTL to RS-485 converter module

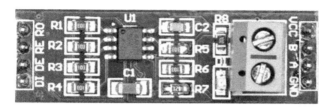

Pin Name	Pin Description
VCC	5V
A	Non-inverting Receiver Input Non-Inverting Driver Output
B	Inverting Receiver Input Inverting Driver Output
GND	GND (0V)
RO	Receiver Out (RX pin)
RE	Receiver Output (LOW-Enable)
DE	Driver Output (HIGH-Enable)
DI	Driver Input (TX pin)

MAX-485 TTL to RS-485 converter module has following highlights:

1. Working voltage: 5V

2. On-board MAX485 chip

3. A low control utilization for the RS485 correspondence

4. Slew-rate constrained handset

5. 5.08mm pitch 2P terminal

6. Helpful RS-485 correspondence wiring

7. Board size: 44 x 14mm

8. It permits sequential correspondence over long separation of 1200 meters

Connecting RS-485 Module with Raspberry Pi 3 B+

To associate the MAX485 TTL to RS-485 Changed over Module to Raspberry Pi the accompanying UART pins of Pi is utilized (GPIO 14, GPIO 15).

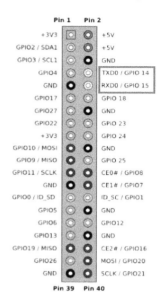

Connecting RS-485 Module with Arduino UNO

To associate the MAX485 TTL to RS-485 Changed over Module to Arduino UNO the accompanying UART pins of UNO is utilized (0,1).

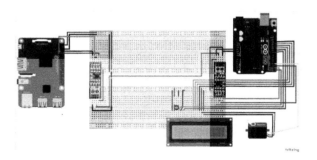

Circuit Connection between one RS-485 and Rasp-

berry Pi 3 B+ (Master):

RS-485	Raspberry Pi 3 B+
DI	GPIO 14 (TX)
DE RE	GPIO4
RO	GPIO 15 (RX)
VCC	5V
GND	GND
A	To A of Slave RS-485
B	To B of Slave RS-485

Circuit Connection between one RS-485 and Arduino UNO (Slave):

RS-485	Arduino UNO
DI	1 (TX)
DE RE	2
RO	0 (RX)
VCC	5V
GND	GND
A	To A of Master RS-485
B	To B of Master RS-485

Arduino UNO with Servo Motor SG-90:

Servo Motor (SG-90)	Arduino UNO
RED	+5V
ORANGE (PWM)	3
BROWN	GND

Circuit Connection between a 16x2 LCD and Arduino UNO:

16x2 LCD	Arduino UNO
VSS	GND
VDD	+5V
V0	To potentiometer centre pin for contrast control of LCD
RS	8
RW	GND
E	9
D4	10
D5	11
D6	12
D7	13
A	+5V
K	GND

This completes all the essential circuit associations between all parts. Presently begin programming the Raspberry Pi as well as Arduino UNO with the Master as well as Slave code.

Programming Raspberry Pi as Master using Python

In the Master Raspberry Pi, the edge estimation of range (0,10,45,90,135,180,135,90,45,10,0) is sent to the RS-485 module by means of sequential port of Pi that sends an incentive to the Arduino UNO and controls the servo engine as per that. In this way, for utilizing Serial port in Raspberry Pi the UART Serial port must be empowered.

Enabling the UART (Serial Port) pins in Raspberry Pi: only bold
Before utilizing UART sticks in Raspberry Pi, it should be empowered. Pursue the means underneath to empower the UART (Serial) Pins in Raspberry Pi board.

1. Open a terminal and type sudo raspi-config

2. Select Interfacing alternatives

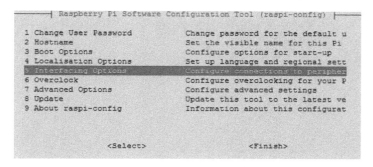

3. And afterward select sequential

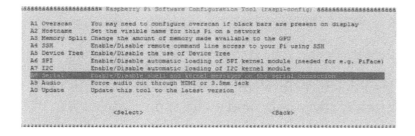

4. At that point click on 'No' (This is utilized to handicap Linux UART reassure)

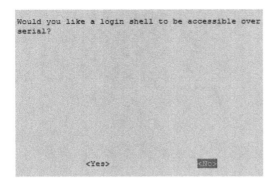

```
Would you like a login shell to be accessible over
serial?




                    <Yes>                    <No>
```

5. After that leave the raspi-config

6. Reboot the Pi

Presently Serial port is prepared to be utilized.

Significant: Before composing esteems to the RS-485 module the pins DE and RE must be made HIGH.

In this way, how about we find in insight concerning Python coding at ace side at this point.

At first, every one of the libraries are imported for peripherals utilized. The libraries which are significant here are time, serial(for sequential correspondence), GPIO for getting to GPIO and rest.

import time

import serial

```
import RPi.GPIO as GPIO
```

```
from time import sleep
```

Underneath, GPIO.BOARD choice indicates that you are alluding to the pins by the quantity of stick in the board.

```
GPIO.setmode(GPIO.BOARD)
```

The GPIO stick number 7 on the Raspberry Pi is made HIGH in light of the fact that the stick 7 of Pi is associated with DE and RE of RS-485. It is made HIGH since it makes RPi to send qualities to RS-485.

```
GPIO.setup(7, GPIO.OUT, initial=GPIO.HIGH)
```

Start the sequential class at the pins GPIO 14 and GPIO 15 (Serial0 Port) with different data like which sequential port, baud rate, equality and stop bits.

```
send = serial.Serial(

    port='/dev/serial0',

    baudrate = 9600,
```

```
    parity=serial.PARITY_NONE,

    stopbits=serial.STOPBITS_ONE,

    bytesize=serial.EIGHTBITS,

    timeout=1

)
```

The variable 'I' with cluster of edge esteems is characterized, these qualities will be sent by means of sequential correspondence.

```
i = [0,10,45,90,135,180,135,90,45,10,0]
```

The capacity send.write(str(x)) sends the qualities to sequential port to the RS-485 individually composed inside the while circle as it executes persistently. The qualities are sent with a deferral of 1.5 seconds.

```
while True:

for x in i:

    send.write(str(x))

    print(x)
```

time.sleep(1.5)

This completes the code for Raspberry Pi which is going about as ace in RS485 based sequential correspondence.

Programming Arduino UNO (Slave)

At the Slave side which is Arduino UNO, the qualities are gotten from the Master. The servo engine associated with Arduino is turned by the worth got, and furthermore the worth is shown in LCD show. In this way, in Arduino programming LCD show library and Servo engine library utilized.

IMPORTANT

As the Slave RS-485 of Arduino UNO gets esteem, the pins DE and RE must be made LOW.

Arduino IDE is utilized for programming Arduino UNO.

Much the same as for ace we had a few peripherals and included vital libraries, likewise the slave side has peripherals, for example, servo engine and 16X2 LCD show, so begin with including libraries for these peripherals.

#include <LiquidCrystal.h>

```
#include <Servo.h>
```

Next the 16X2 LCD show sticks that are to be utilized with the Arduino UNO are characterized and afterward the Servo article is additionally made.

```
LiquidCrystal lcd(8,9,10,11,12,13);      // Define
LCD display pins RS,E,D4,D5,D6,D7

Servo servo;
```

At first a presentation message is shown which can be changed by the task and after that it is cleared for next message.

```
lcd.begin(16,2);

lcd.print("Hello_world");

lcd.setCursor(0,1);

lcd.print("RS_485");

delay(3000);

lcd.clear();
```

The sequential correspondence is begun at baud pace

of 9600.

> **Serial.begin(9600);**

As Arduino RS-485 gets an incentive from ace, so the stick 2 of (EnablePin) is made LOW to make it in info mode and furthermore to make stick DE and RE of RS-485 LOW to peruse an incentive from Master Raspberry Pi.

> **digitalWrite(enablePin, LOW);**

The Servo Motor PWM stick is associated with the Arduino PWM stick 3.

> **servo.attach(3);**

The while circle executes when there is a worth accessible at sequential port where RS485 module is associated.

The Serial.paseInt() work is utilized to get the whole number worth (Angle) from sequential port that is sent from Raspberry Pi

> **int angle = Serial.parseInt();**

Anbazhagan k

Compose the got edge an incentive to servo engine to turn the servo engine shaft from (0 to 180).

```
servo.write(angle);
```

Lastly, the point worth is shown in LCD show utilizing the particular LCD capacities.

```
lcd.setCursor(0,0);

    lcd.print("Angle From RPi ");

    lcd.setCursor(0,1);

    lcd.print(angle);
```

This completes the slave side programming. Likewise with transferring the codes in Raspberry Pi promotion Arduino UNO, both the controllers are prepared for a working demo.

Testing the RS 485 Serial communication with Raspberry Pi and Arduino UNO

At the point when circuit associations are finished and code is transferred to Arduino UNO, at that point utilize terminal to run the python code in Raspberry Pi. The Angle worth is sent from Raspberry Pi to Arduino Uno to control the Servo Motor point by means

Arduino and Raspberry Pi Best informative Projects for future of RS-485 Serial Communication.

1. At Angle: 0

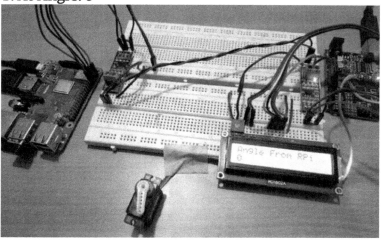

2. At Angle: 90

3. At Angle:135

4. At Angle:180

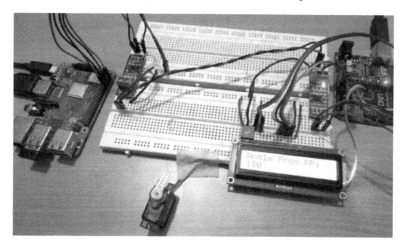

This completes the total instructional exercise on RS485 sequential correspondence utilizing Raspberry Pi..

Code

Master Raspberry Pi Code:

```
import time
import serial
import RPi.GPIO as GPIO
from time import sleep
GPIO.setwarnings(False)
GPIO.setmode(GPIO.BOARD)
GPIO.setup(7, GPIO.OUT, initial=GPIO.HIGH)
send = serial.Serial(
  port='/dev/serial0',
  baudrate = 9600,
  parity=serial.PARITY_NONE,
  stopbits=serial.STOPBITS_ONE,
```

```
  bytesize=serial.EIGHTBITS,
  timeout=1
)
i = [0,10,45,90,135,180,135,90,45,10,0]
while True:
for x in i:
  send.write(str(x))
  print(x)
  time.sleep(1.5)
```

Slave Arduino Code:

```
#include <LiquidCrystal.h>          //Include LCD
library for using LCD display functions
#include <Servo.h>          //For using Servo functions
int enablePin = 2;
LiquidCrystal lcd(8,9,10,11,12,13);          // Define LCD
display pins RS,E,D4,D5,D6,D7
Servo servo;
void setup()
{
 lcd.begin(16,2);
 lcd.print("Helloworld");
 lcd.setCursor(0,1);
 lcd.print("RS_485");
 delay(3000);
 lcd.clear();
 Serial.begin(9600);          // initialize serial at bau-
drate 9600:
 pinMode(enablePin, OUTPUT);
 delay(10);
 digitalWrite(enablePin, LOW);          // (Pin 2 always
```

LOW to receive value from Master)

```
 servo.attach(3);          // (Servo PWM pin connected
to Pin 3 PWM pin of Arduino)
}
void loop()
{
 while (Serial.available())        //While have data at
Serial port this loop executes
  {


     lcd.clear();
   int angle = Serial.parseInt();     //Receive INTEGER
value from Master throught RS-485
   servo.write(angle);              //Write received value
to Servo PWM pin (Setting Angle)
   lcd.setCursor(0,0);
   lcd.print("Angle From RPi ");
   lcd.setCursor(0,1);
   lcd.print(angle);             //Displays the Angle value


  }
}
```

6.ARDUINO 7 SEGMENT DISPLAY CLOCK BY MULTIPLEXING FOUR 7 SEGMENT DISPLAYS

Computerized divider Clocks are getting increasingly famous now days and they are superior to anything simple clock as it gives exact time in hours, minutes and seconds and its simple to peruse the qualities. Some advanced tickers likewise have numerous offices like showing temperature, stickiness, setting various alerts and so on. The large majority of the advanced tickers utilize seven section show.

We recently assembled numerous advanced tickers circuits either utilizing 7 fragment shows or utilizing 16x2 LCD. Here you can the total PCB structures of AVR based Digital clock. This instructional exercise is tied in with making a Digital clock by multiplexing four-7 section presentations utilizing Arduino UNO and showing the time in HH:MM position.

Components Required

1. 74HC595 IC
2. 4-Digit 7 Segment Display
3. Arduino UNO
4. DS3231 RTC Module
5. Connecting wires
6. Breadboard

4-Digit 7 Segment Display

four-digit seven Segment show has four seven frag-ment show consolidated or we can say multiplexed together. They are utilized to show numerical qual-ities and furthermore a few letters in order with deci-mals and colon. The showcase can be utilized both way. Four digits are valuable for making computer-ized tickers or like checking numbers from 0 to 9999. The following is the inner graph for 4-Digit 7 Segment show.

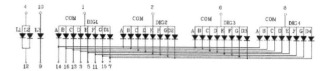

Each section has one LED with individual LED control. There are two kinds of seven portion shows, for example, Common Anode and Common Cathode. The above picture demonstrates the normal anode type 7 section show.

Common Anode

In like manner anode all the positive terminals anodes of all the eight leds is combined both, named as COM. And all the negative terminals is disregarded or associated with the microcontroller pins. By utilizing microcontroller, if rationale LOW is set to light up the specific LED fragment and set rationale High to mood killer LED.

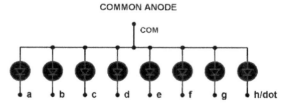

Internal connections of 7 Segment COMMON ANODE Display

Common Cathode

In Common Cathode, all the Negative terminals (cathode) of all the eight LEDs is combined both, named as COM. All the positive terminals are disregarded or associated with the microcontroller pins. By utilizing microcontroller, whenever set rationale HIGH to enlighten the LED and set LOW to mood killer LED.

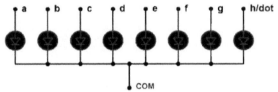

COMMON CATHODE

Internal connections of 7 Segment COMMON CATHODE Display

Study 7 fragment shows here and check how it tends to be interfaced with different microcontrollers:

1. 7 Segment Display Interfacing with Arduino

2. 7 Segment Display Interfacing with Raspberry Pi

3. Interfacing Seven Segment Display with ARM7-LPC2148

4. 7 Segment Display Interfacing with PIC Microcontroller

5. 7 Segment Display Interfacing with 8051 Microcontroller

74HC595 Shift Register IC

74HC595

1	Q1	Vcc	16
2	Q2	Q0	15
3	Q3	DS	14
4	Q4	OE	13
5	Q5	ST_CP	12
6	Q6	SH_CP	11
7	Q7	MR	10
8	GND	Q7'	9

The IC 74HC595 otherwise called 8-Bit Serial IN – Parallel OUT Shift Register. This IC can get information contribution to sequential and can control 8 yield sticks in parallel. This is valuable in lessening pins utilized from microcontroller. You can discover all the 74HC595 move register related tasks here.

Working of 74HC595 IC:

This IC utilizes three sticks, for example, Clock, Data and Latch with the microcontroller to control the 8 yield pins of the IC. The clock is utilized to give constantly beats from microcontroller and information stick is utilized to send the information like which yield should be turned ON or OFF at the individual clock time.

Pinout:

Pin Number	Pin Name	Description
1,2,3,4,5,6,7	Output Pins (Q1 to Q7)	The 74HC595 has 8 output pins out of which 7 are these pins. They can be controlled serially
8	Ground	Connected to the Ground of microcontroller
9	(Q7) Serial Output	This pin is used to connect more than one 74HC595 as cascading
10	(MR) Master Reset	Resets all outputs as low. Must be held high for normal operation
11	(SH_CP) Clock	This is the clock pin to which the clock signal has to be provided from MCU/MPU
12	(ST_CP) Latch	The Latch pin is used to update the data to the output pins. It is active high

13	(OE) Output Enable	The Output Enable is used to turn off the outputs. Must be held low for normal operation
14	(DS) Serial Data	This is the pin to which data is sent, based on which the 8 outputs are controlled
15	(Q0) Output	The first output pin.
16	Vcc	This pin powers the IC, typically +5V is used.

DS3231 RTC Module

DS3231 is a RTC module. RTC represents Real Time Clock. This module is utilized to recollect the time and date notwithstanding when the circuit isn't controlled. It has a battery reinforcement CR2032 to run the module without outer power. This module likewise incorporates a temperature sensor. The module can be utilized in installed ventures, for example, making advanced clock with temperature marker and so on. Here are some valuable tasks utilizing it:

1. Programmed Pet Feeder utilizing Arduino

2. Interfacing RTC Module (DS3231) with PIC Microcontroller: Digital Clock

3. Interfacing RTC module (DS3231) with MSP430: Digital Clock

4. ESP32 Real Time Clock utilizing DS3231 Module

5. Advanced Wall Clock on PCB utilizing AVR Microcontroller Atmega16 as well as DS3231 RTC

Pinout of DS3231:

Pin Name	Use
VCC	Connected to positive of power source
GND	Connected to ground
SDA	Serial data pin (I2C)
SCL	Serial clock pin (I2C)
SQW	Square Wave output pin
32K	32K oscillator output

Features & Specifications:

· RTC checks seconds, minutes, hours and year

· Advanced temperature sensor with ±3ºC

exactness

- Register for Aging trim

- 400Khz I2C interface

- Low control utilization

- CR2032 battery reinforcement with a multi year life

- Working Voltage: 2.3 to 5.5V

Circuit Diagram

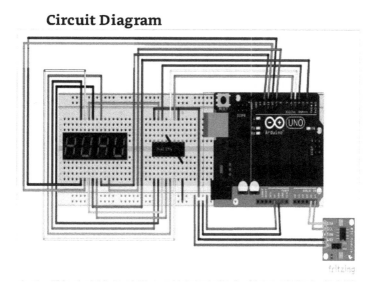

Circuit Connection between DS3231 RTC & Arduino UNO:

DS3231	Arduino UNO
VCC	5V
GND	GND
SDA	A4
SCL	A4

Circuit Connections between 74HC595 IC & Arduino Uno:

74HC595 IC	Arduino UNO
11-SH_CP (SRCLK)	6
12-ST_CP (RCLK)	5
14-DS (Data)	4
13-OE(Latch)	GND
8-GND	GND
10-MR(SRCLR)	+5V
16-VCC	+5V

Circuit Connections between IC 74HC595 & 4-Digit Seven Segment & Arduino UNO:

4-DigitSevenSegment	IC 74HC595	Arduino UNO
A	Q0	-
B	Q1	-

C	Q2	-
D	Q3	-
E	Q4	-
F	Q5	-
G	Q6	-
D1	-	10
D2	-	11
D3	-	12
D4	-	9

Programming Arduino UNO for Multiplexing Seven Segment Display

The total code is joined toward the part of the bargain. In the programming segment, how the time (hour and moment) is taken from the RTC module in 24hr arrangement and after that it is changed over into particular configuration for showing them in the tetra-digit heptad Segment show will be clarified.

To interface the DS3231 RTC module with Arduino UNO the I2C transport of Arduino UNO is utilized. A library called <DS3231.h> is incorporated into the program to access capacities like setting and perusing time, date, temperature information and so forth. Download the DS3231 RTC module Arduino Library. As RTC module utilizes I2C interface the <wire.h> library is additionally utilized in the program.

In this idea, hour and moment is taken first from RTC as well as they are combined both like 0930 (09:30 pm) as well as after that the individual digits is isolated like thousand, hundred, tens, unit and the individual digits changed over into paired organization like 0 into 63 (0111111). This double code is sent to a move register and afterward from the move register to the seven-section, effectively showing the Digit 0 out of seven fragment show. Along these lines, the four digits are multiplexed and hour and moment is shown.

At first, the important library is incorporated, for example, DS3231 library and Wire library(I2C library).

```
#include <Wire.h>
```

```
#include<DS3231.h>
```

The pins are characterized for the seven fragment control. These controls will assume significant job in multiplexing the showcase.

```
#define latchPin 5

#define clockPin 6

#define dataPin 4

#define dot 2
```

The factors are proclaimed to store the changed over or crude outcome taken from the RTC.

```
int h;       //Variable declared for hour

int m;       //Variable declared for minute

int thousands;

int hundreds;

int tens;

int unit;
```

```
bool h24;

bool PM;
```

Next the item for the class DS3231 is proclaimed as RTC to disentangle the utilization in further lines.

```
DS3231 RTC;
```

As RTC module is interfaced with Arduino by utilizing I2C correspondence. Along these lines, wire.begin() is utilized to begin I2C correspondence in default address of RTC as there are no other I2C modules.

```
Wire.begin();
```

The stick mode are characterized, regardless of whether the GPIO will carry on as yield or information.

```
pinMode(9,OUTPUT);

  pinMode(10,OUTPUT);

  pinMode(11,OUTPUT);

  pinMode(12,OUTPUT);
```

```
pinMode(latchPin, OUTPUT);

pinMode(clockPin, OUTPUT);

pinMode(dataPin, OUTPUT);

pinMode(dot,OUTPUT);
```

The circle runs endlessly and it requires some investment in hour and moment from the RTC DS3231 module. 'h24' demonstrates the 24hr organization variable.

```
int h= RTC.getHour(h24, PM);

int m = RTC.getMinute();
```

At that point the hour and moment is joined as one number (model in the event that hour is 10 and min is 60, at that point number is 10*100=1000+60 =1060).

```
int number = h*100+m;
```

The individual digits from number are gotten (model 1060-1 is thousand,0 is hundered,1 is tenth and 0 is last digit). To isolate the digits, modulus administrator is utilized. For instance, in 1060 to get 1 then 1060/1000=1.06%10=1). So isolated digits are put away in discrete factors.

```
int thousands = number/1000%10;

int hundreds = number/100%10;

int tens = number/10%10;

int unit = number%10;
```

After that a switch case explanation for every individual digit is characterized for changing over them into particular configuration (paired arrangement) and conveying by means of move register to show in 7-portion. For instance (For 1 digit it is changed into 06 (0000 0110)). With the goal that it is conveyed by means of move and 1 digit is shown in 7-section (0 for LOW, 1 for HIGH).

```
switch (t)

{

  case 0:

  unit = 63;

  break;
```

```
case 1:

unit = 06;

 break;

case 2:

unit =91;

 break;

case 3:

unit=79;

 break;

case 4:

unit=102;

 break;

case 5:

unit = 109;

 break;
```

```
case 6:

unit =125;

case 7:

unit = 07;

break;

case 8:

unit = 127;

break;

case 9:

unit =103;

break;

}
```

At that point the individual digit in parallel configuration is conveyed by means of 'shiftout' work with
MSB first and the separate digit stick is made HIGH
and lock stick is made HIGH.

```
digitalWrite(9, LOW);

  digitalWrite(latchPin, LOW);

  shiftOut(dataPin,   clockPin,   MSBFIRST,thou-
sands);

  digitalWrite(latchPin, HIGH);

  digitalWrite(9, HIGH);

  delay(5);
```

This completes the total code. A large portion of the capacity clarification are given in the code remark segment just next to the code line. The recurrence of the clock will choose the perspective on Time and nature of multiplexing I.e. in the event that low clock is utilized, at that point the flashing can be considered where to be in case that the clock speed is high, at that point there won't be such glimmering and an enduring time can be seen.

Note that to get to the RTC module, the I2C transport voltage must be kept up.

Code

//Four-Digit 7 Segments Multiplexing using Arduino: Display time in HH:MM

```
#include <Wire.h>   //Library for SPI communication
#include <DS3231.h> //Library for RTC module
#define latchPin 5
#define clockPin 6
#define dataPin 4
#define dot 2
DS3231 RTC;     //Declare object RTC for class DS3231
int h;       //Variable declared for hour
int m;        //Variable declared for minute
int thousands;
int hundreds;
int tens;
int unit;
bool h24;
bool PM;
```

```
void setup ()
{
  Wire.begin();
  pinMode(9,OUTPUT);
  pinMode(10,OUTPUT);
  pinMode(11,OUTPUT);
  pinMode(12,OUTPUT);
  pinMode(latchPin, OUTPUT);
  pinMode(clockPin, OUTPUT);
  pinMode(dataPin, OUTPUT);
  pinMode(dot,OUTPUT);
}


void loop ()
{
  digitalWrite(dot,HIGH);
  int h= RTC.getHour(h24, PM); //To get the Hour
  int m = RTC.getMinute();   //TO get the minute
    int number = h*100+m;        //Converts hour and
minute in 4-digit
    int thousands = number/1000%10; //Getting thou-
sands digit from the 4 digit
    int hundreds = number/100%10;  //Getting hun-
dreds digit from 4 digit
    int tens = number/10%10;      //Getting tens digit
from 4-digit
    int unit = number%10;        //Getting last digit from
4-digit
  int t= unit;
  int u= tens;
```

```
 int v= hundreds;
 int w= thousands;
```

//Converting the individual digits into corresponding number for passing it through the shift register so LEDs are turned ON or OFF in seven segment

```
switch (t)
{
 case 0:
 unit = 63;
 break;
 case 1:
 unit = 06;
 break;
 case 2:
 unit =91;
 break;
 case 3:
 unit=79;
 break;
 case 4:
 unit=102;
 break;
 case 5:
 unit = 109;
 break;
 case 6:
 unit =125;
 case 7:
 unit = 07;
 break;
 case 8:
```

```
 unit = 127;
 break;
 case 9:
 unit =103;
 break;
 }
switch (u)
{
 case 0:
 tens = 63;
 break;
 case 1:
 tens = 06;
 break;
 case 2:
 tens =91;
 break;
 case 3:
 tens=79;
 break;
 case 4:
 tens=102;
 break;
 case 5:
 tens= 109;
 break;
 case 6:
 tens =125;
 case 7:
 tens = 07;
 break;
```

```
case 8:
tens = 127;
break;
case 9:
tens = 103;
break;
}


 switch (v)
{
case 0:
hundreds = 63;
break;
case 1:
hundreds = 06;
break;
case 2:
hundreds = 91;
break;
case 3:
hundreds = 79;
break;
case 4:
hundreds = 102;
break;
case 5:
hundreds = 109;
break;
case 6:
hundreds = 125;
```

```
case 7:
hundreds = 07;
break;
case 8:
hundreds = 127;
break;
case 9:
hundreds =103;
break;
}


 switch (w)
{
case 0:
thousands = 63;
break;
case 1:
thousands = 06;
break;
case 2:
thousands =91;
break;
case 3:
thousands=79;
break;
case 4:
thousands=102;
break;
case 5:
thousands = 109;
```

```
break;
case 6:
thousands =125;
case 7:
thousands = 07;
break;
case 8:
thousands= 127;
break;
case 9:
thousands =103;
break;
}
   digitalWrite(9, LOW);
 digitalWrite(latchPin, LOW);
      shiftOut(dataPin, clockPin, MSBFIRST,thousands); // The thousand digit is sent
 digitalWrite(latchPin, HIGH); // Set latch pin HIGH
to store the inputs
 digitalWrite(9, HIGH);      // Turinig on that thousands digit
 delay(5);          // delay for multiplexing
   digitalWrite(10, LOW);
 digitalWrite(latchPin, LOW);
      shiftOut(dataPin, clockPin, MSBFIRST,hundreds ); // The hundered digit is sent
 digitalWrite(latchPin, HIGH);
 digitalWrite(10, HIGH);
 delay(5);
```

```
    digitalWrite(11, LOW);
  digitalWrite(latchPin, LOW);
   shiftOut(dataPin, clockPin, MSBFIRST,tens);  // The
tens digit is sent
  digitalWrite(latchPin, HIGH);
  digitalWrite(11, HIGH);
  delay(5);


    digitalWrite(12, LOW);
  digitalWrite(latchPin, LOW);
   shiftOut(dataPin, clockPin, MSBFIRST,unit);  // The
last digit is sent
  digitalWrite(latchPin, HIGH);
  digitalWrite(12, HIGH);
  delay(5);


}
```

7.CONTROL HOME LIGHTS WITH TOUCH USING TTP223 TOUCH SENSOR AND ARDUINO UNO

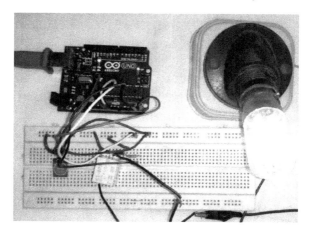

In certain applications, client information is required to control the elements of a gadget. There are various types of client input strategies utilized in the implanted and computerized gadgets. The touch sensor is one of them. Contact sensor is a significant and broadly utilized information gadget to interface with a microcontroller and it has made contributing information less complex. There are individual spots where the touch sensor can be utilized, regardless of whether it very well may be a cell phone or a LCD screen switch. Be that as it may, there are numerous kinds of sensors accessible in the market however Capacitive touch sensor is the broadly utilized sort in contact sensor fragment.

In the past instructional exercise, we have done Controlling Light utilizing Touch Sensor and 8051 Microcontroller, Now in this undertaking, a similar touch sensor will be interfaced with Arduino UNO. The Arduino is a generally mainstream and effectively accessible improvement board.

We recently utilized touch based information strategies utilizing capacitive touch cushions with various microcontrollers, for example,

- Contact Keypad Interfacing with ATmega32 Microcontroller

- Capacitive Touch Pad with Raspberry Pi

Touch Sensor

The touch sensor, which will be utilized for this undertaking is a capacitive touch sensor module and the sensor driver depends on the driver IC TTP223. The working voltage of the TTP223 IC is from the 2 V to 5.5 V and the present utilization of the touch sensor is exceptionally low. Due to the modest, low current utilization, and simple to incorporate help, the touch sensor with TTP223 ends up famous in the capacitive touch sensor portion.

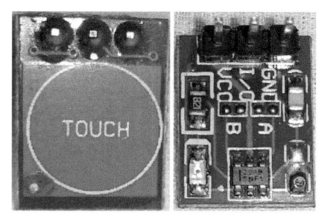

In the above picture, the two sides of the sensor are indicated where the pinout outline is plainly unmistakable. It likewise has a patch jumper which can be utilized to reconfigure the sensor in regard of the yield. The jumper is An and B. Default arrangement or in the default condition of the bind jumper, the yield changes from LOW to HIGH when the sensor is contacted. Be that as it may, when the jumper is set and the sensor is reconfigured, the yield changes its state when the touch sensor identifies the touch. The affectability of the touch sensor can be additionally arranged by changing the capacitor. For the point-wise info,go through the datasheet of the TTP 223 which will be extremely helpful.

Underneath outline is demonstrating various yields at various jumper settings-

Jumper A	Jumper B	Output Lock State	Output TTL level
Open	Open	No-lock	High
Open	Close	Self-lock	High
Close	Open	No-Lock	Low
Close	Close	Self-Lock	Low

For this undertaking, the sensor will be utilized as the default design which is accessible on the manufacturing plant discharge condition.

Machines can be constrained by utilizing the touch sensor, and by interfacing it with a microcontroller. In this task, the touch sensor will be utilized to control a Light Bulb as ON or OFF utilizing Arduino UNO and Relay.

Get to know about Relay

To interface the transfer, it is critical to have a reasonable thought regarding the hand-off's stick depiction. The pinout of the hand-off can be found in the underneath picture

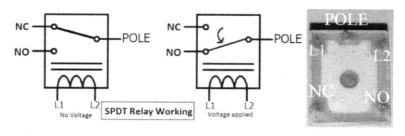

NO is regularly open and NC is typically associated. L1 as well as L2 are the two terminals of the Relay loop. At the point when the Voltage isn't connected, the transfer is killed and the POLE gets associated with the NC stick. At the point when the voltage is connected over the curl terminals, L1 and L2 of the transfer gets turned ON and the POLE gets associated with the NO. In this way, the association among POLE and NO can be changed to ON or OFF by changing the tasks condition of the Relay. It is profoundly fitting to check the hand-off particular before the application. The hand-off has a working voltage over the L1 and L2. Some hand-off works with 12V, some with the 6V and some with the 5V. Not just has this, the NO, NC and POLE additionally had a voltage and current rating. For this application, we are utilizing 5V Relay with 250V, 6A rating on the exchanging side.

Components Required

1. Arduino UNO
2. The USB cable for programming and power
3. Standard Cubic Relay - 5V
4. 2k resistor - 1 pc

5. 4.7k resistor - 1 pc
6. light with bulb holder
7. loads of hookup wires or berg wires
8. TTP223 Sensor module
9. BC549B transistor
10. 1N4007 Diode
11. A telephone charger to associate the Arduino via USB cable.
12. A breadboard
13. Arduino programming platform.

2k resistor, BC549B, 1N4007, as well as the Relay can be supplanted with a Relay Module.

Circuit Diagram

The schematic for interfacing contact sensor with Arduino is basic and can be seen underneath,

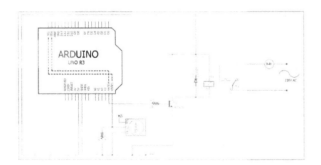

The transistor is utilized to turn on or off the Relay. This is because of the Arduino GPIO pins are not skilled to give enough current to drive the Relay. The

1N4007 is required for EMI closing during Relay on or off circumstance. The diode is going about as a free-wheel diode. The touch sensor is associated with the Arduino UNO board.

The circuit is built on a breadboard with the Arduino as underneath.

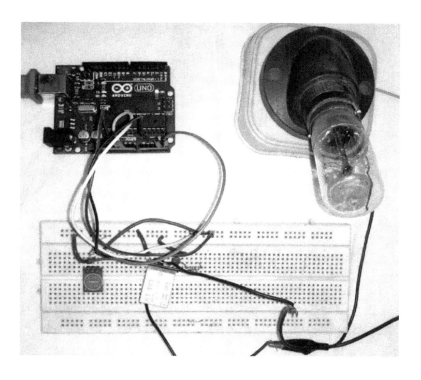

The correct breadboard association can be found in the underneath schematic.

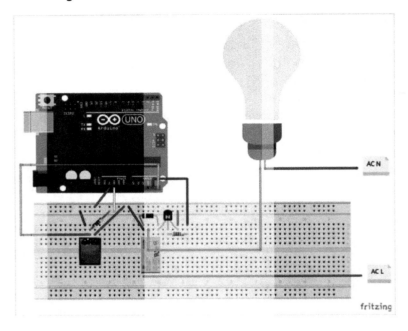

fritzing

Programming Arduino UNO to Control Light Bulb using Touch Sensor

Complete program is given toward the end. Here we are clarifying couple of significant pieces of the code. The Arduino UNO will be modified utilizing Arduino IDE. Initially, the Arduino library is incorporated to get to all default elements of Arduino.

```
#include <Arduino.h>
```

Characterize all the stick numbers where hand-off and contact sensor will be associated. Here, the touch sensor is associated with stick A5. The inbuilt LED is additionally utilized which is legitimately associated in the board to stick 13. The hand-off is associated with stick A4.

```
/*

* Pin Description

*/

int Touch_Sensor = A5;

int LED = 13;

int Relay = A4;
```

Characterize the stick mode for example what ought to be the stick work whether as information or yield. Here touch sensor is made information. Transfer and LED pins are yield.

```
/*

* Pin mode setup

*/
```

```
void setup() {

        pinMode(Touch_Sensor, INPUT);

        pinMode(LED, OUTPUT);

        pinMode(Relay, OUTPUT);

}
```

Two whole numbers are proclaimed where the 'condition' is utilized to hold the sensor's condition whether it is contacted or not. The 'state' is utilized for holding the condition of the LED and Relay, on or off.

```
/*

* Programme flow Description

*/

int condition = 0;

int state = 0; //To hold the switch state.
```

The touch sensor changes the rationale 0 to 1 when it is contacted. This is perused by the digitalRead() work and the worth is put away in the condition variable. At the point when the condition is 1, the condition of the LED and Relay gets changed. Be that as it may, to recognize the touch precisely, a debounce deferral is utilized. The debounce delay, delay(250); is utilized to affirm the single touch.

```
void loop() {

        condition = digitalRead(A5); // Reading
digital data from the A5 Pin of the Arduino.

        if(condition == 1){

                delay(250); // de-bounce delay.

                if(condition == 1){

                        state = ~state; // Changing
the state of the switch.

                        digitalWrite(LED, state);

                        digitalWrite(Relay, state);

                }

        }

}
```

Testing the Working of Touch Sensor TTP223

The circuit is tried in the breadboard with a low control bulb associated with it.

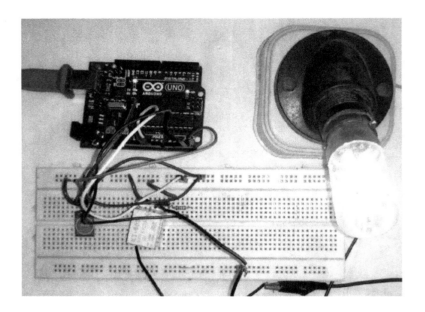

Note that this task utilizes 230-240V AC voltage, so it is encouraged to be cautious while utilizing bulb.

Code

```
/*//
=======================================
===================================//
 * TTP223 interfacing with Arduino
 *///
```

```
=========================================
====================================//
#include <Arduino.h>
//#define ON 1
//#define OFF 0
/*
 * Pin Description
 */
int Touch_Sensor = A5;
int LED = 13;
int Relay = A4;
/*
 * Programme flow Description
 */
int condition = 0;
int state = 0; //To hold the switch state.
/*
 * Pin mode setup
 */
void setup() {
pinMode(Touch_Sensor, INPUT);
pinMode(LED, OUTPUT);
pinMode(Relay, OUTPUT);
}
void loop() {
condition = digitalRead(A5); // Reading digital data
from the A5 Pin of the Arduino.
if(condition == 1){
delay(250); // de-bounce delay.
if(condition == 1){
state = ~state; // Changing the state of the switch.
```

```
digitalWrite(LED, state);
digitalWrite(Relay, state);
}
}
}
```

8.HOW TO USE OV7670 CAMERA MODULE WITH ARDUINO

How to Use OV7670
Camera Module
with Arduino

Cameras have constantly ruled the gadgets business as it has heaps of uses, for example, guest observing framework, observation framework, participation framework and so forth. Cameras that we use today are keen and have a great deal of highlights that were absent in prior cameras. While todays advanced cameras catch pictures as well as catches abnormal state depictions of the scene and break down what they see. It is utilized broadly in Robotics, Artificial Intelligence, Machine Learning and so on. The Captured casings are prepared utilizing Artificial Intelligence and Machine Learning, and afterward utilized in numerous applications like Number plate location, object discovery, movement identification, facial acknowledgment and so forth.

In this instructional exercise we will interface most

generally utilized camera module OV7670 with Arduino UNO. The camera module OV7670 can be interfaced with Arduino Mega with similar stick design, code and steps. The camera module is difficult to interface since it has enormous number of pins and confused wiring to do. Additionally the wire turns to be significant when utilizing camera modules as the decision of the wire and length of the wire can essentially influence the image quality and can bring commotion.

We have effectively done plentiful ventures on Cameras with various sort of Microcontrollers and IoT Devices, for example,

- Guest Monitoring System with Raspberry Pi and Pi Camera

- IOT based Raspberry Pi Home Security System with Email Alert

- Raspberry Pi Surveillance Camera with Motion Capture

The Camera OV7670 chips away at 3.3V, so it turns out to be critical to stay away from Arduino which gives 5V yield at their Output GPIO pins. The OV7670 is a FIFO camera. Be that as it may, in this instructional exercise, the image or casings will be gotten without FIFO. This instructional exercise will have straightforward advances and disentangled programming to interface OV7670 with Arduino UNO.

Components Required

1. Arduino UNO
2. OV7670 Camera Module
3. Resistors(10k, 4.7k)
4. Jumpers

Software Required:

1. Arduino IDE
2. Sequential Port Reader (To dissect Output Image)

Things to Remember about Camera Module OV7670

OV7670 Camera Module is a FIFO camera Module accessible from various Manufacturers with various stick Configurations. TheOV7670 gives full outline, windowed 8-piece pictures in a wide scope of configurations. The picture cluster is equipped for working at up to 30 edges for each second (fps) in VGA. The OV7670 incorporates

1. Picture Sensor Array(of around 656 x 488 pixels)

2. Timing Generator

3. Simple Signal Processor

4. A/D Converters

5. Test Pattern Generator

6. Advanced Signal Processor(DSP)

7. Picture Scaler

8. Advanced Video Port

9. Driven and Strobe Flash Control Output

The OV7670 picture sensor is controlled utilizing Serial Camera Control Bus (SCCB) which is an I2C interface (SIOC, SIOD) with a most extreme clock recurrence of 400KHz.

The Camera accompanies handshaking sign, for example,

- **VSYNC:** Vertical Sync Output – Low during casing

- **HREF:** Horizontal Reference – High during dynamic pixels of line

- **PCLK:** Pixel Clock Output – Free running clock. Information is legitimate on rising edge

What's more, it has a few additional sign, for example,

- **D0-D7:** 8-piece YUV/RGB Video Component Digital Output

- **PWDN:** Power Down Mode Selection – Normal Mode as well as Power Down Mode

- **XCLK:** System Clock Input

- **Reset:** Reset Signal

The OV7670 is timed from a 24MHz oscillator. This gives a Pixel Clock(PCLK) yield of 24MHz. The FIFO gives 3Mbps of video casing support memory. The test design generator highlights 8-bar shading bar design, blur to-dark shading bar patter. Presently how about we begin programming the Arduino UNO for testing Camera OV7670 and snatching edges utilizing sequential port peruser.

Circuit Diagram

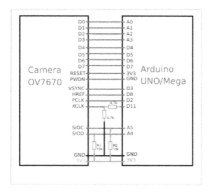

Programming Arduino UNO

The programming begins with including required library essential for OV7670. Since OV7670 keeps running on I2C interface, it incorporates <util/twi.h> library. The libraries utilized in this venture are worked in libraries of ArduinoIDE. We simply need to incorporate the libraries to take care of business.

After this, the registers should be altered for OV7670. The program is isolated into little works for better understanding.

The Setup() involves all the underlying arrangements required for just picture catching. The main capacity is arduinoUnoInut() which is utilized to initialise the arduino uno. At first it impairs all the worldwide hinders and sets the correspondence interface setups, for example, the PWM clock, choice of intrude on pins, presclaer determination, including equality and stop bits.

arduinoUnoInut();

In the wake of arranging the Arduino, the camera must be designed. To initialise the camera, we just have the alternatives to change the register esteems. The register esteems should be transformed from the default to the custom. Additionally include required postponement relying on the microcontroller recurrence we are utilizing. As, slow microcontrollers have less preparing time including more postponement between catching casings.

```
void camInit(void){

writeReg(0x12, 0x80);

 _delay_ms(100);

 wrSensorRegs8_8(ov7670_default_regs);

writeReg(REG_COM10, 32);//PCLK does not toggle on HBLANK.

}
```

The camera is set to take a QVGA picture so the goals should be chosen. The capacity designs the register to take a QVGA picture.

setResolution();

In this instructional exercise, the pictures are taken in monochrome, so the register worth is set to yield a monochrome picture. The capacity sets the register esteems from register list which is predefined in the program.

setColor();

The beneath capacity is write to enroll work which composes the hex an incentive to enlist. In the event that you get the mixed pictures, at that point attempt to change the second term for example 10 to 9/11/12. In any case, mostly than not this worth works fine so no compelling reason to transform it.

writeReg(0x11, 10);

This capacity is utilized to get the picture goals size. In this task we are taking pictures in the size of 320 x 240 pixels.

> **captureImg(320, 240);**

Other than this, the code additionally has the I2C arrangements partitioned in to a few sections. Just to get the information from camera, the I2C arrangements has Start, Read, Write, Set Address work which are significant when utilizing I2C convention.

You can locate the total code toward the part of the bargain. Simply Upload the code and open the Serial Port Reader and get the edges.

How to Use Serial Port Reader for reading Images

Sequential Port Reader is a basic GUI, download it from here. This catches the base64 encode and translates it to frame a picture. Simply pursue these straightforward strides to utilize Serial Port Reader

Stage 1: Connect Your Arduino to any USB Port of your PC

Stage 2: Click on "Check" to discover your Arduino COM Port

Stage 3: Finally click on "Begin" catch to begin perusing sequentially.

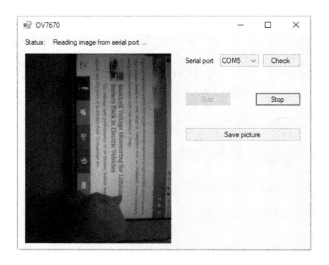

Stage 4: One can likewise spare this photos by simply tapping on "Spare Picture".

Below are Sample Images Taken from the OV7670

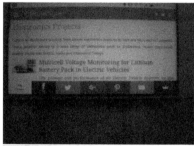

Precautions when using OV7670

1. Attempt to utilize wires or jumpers as short as could be expected under the circumstances

2. Stay away from any free contact to any pins on Arduino or OV7670

3. Be cautious about associating as huge number of wiring can lead cut off

4. On the off chance that the UNO gives 5V yield to GPIO, at that point utilize Level Shifter.

5. Utilize 3.3V Input for OV7670 as surpassing voltage than this can harm the OV7670 module.

This venture is made to give diagram of utilizing a camera module with Arduino. Since Arduino has less memory, so the handling may not be true to form. You can utilize various controllers which has more memory for handling.

Code
```
#include <stdint.h>
#include <avr/io.h>
```

```c
#include <util/twi.h>
#include <util/delay.h>
#include <avr/pgmspace.h>
#define F_CPU 16000000UL
#define vga  0
#define qvga 1
#define qqvga  2
#define yuv422 0
#define rgb565 1
#define bayerRGB 2
#define camAddr_WR 0x42
#define camAddr_RD 0x43
/* Registers */
#define REG_GAIN   0x00 /* Gain lower 8 bits (rest in
vref) */
#define REG_BLUE  0x01 /* blue gain */
#define REG_RED   0x02 /* red gain */
#define REG_VREF   0x03 /* Pieces of GAIN, VSTART,
VSTOP */
#define REG_COM1  0x04 /* Control 1 */
#define COM1_CCIR656 0x40   /* CCIR656 enable */
#define REG_BAVE  0x05 /* U/B Average level */
#define REG_GbAVE  0x06 /* Y/Gb Average level */
#define REG_AECHH  0x07 /* AEC MS 5 bits */
#define REG_RAVE  0x08 /* V/R Average level */
#define REG_COM2  0x09 /* Control 2 */
#define COM2_SSLEEP     0x10 /* Soft sleep mode */
#define REG_PID     0x0a /* Product ID MSB */
#define REG_VER      0x0b /* Product ID LSB */
#define REG_COM3  0x0c /* Control 3 */
```

```
#define COM3_SWAP      0x40 /* Byte swap */
#define COM3_SCALEEN    0x08 /* Enable scaling */
#define COM3_DCWEN     0x04 /* Enable downsamp/
crop/window */
#define REG_COM4  0x0d /* Control 4 */
#define REG_COM5  0x0e /* All "reserved" */
#define REG_COM6  0x0f /* Control 6 */
#define REG_AECH  0x10 /* More bits of AEC value */
#define REG_CLKRC  0x11 /* Clocl control */
#define CLK_EXT       0x40 /* Use external clock dir-
ectly */
#define CLK_SCALE  0x3f /* Mask for internal clock
scale */
#define REG_COM7   0x12 /* Control 7 */ //REG mean
address.
#define COM7_RESET      0x80 /* Register reset */
#define COM7_FMT_MASK     0x38
#define COM7_FMT_VGA     0x00
#define COM7_FMT_CIF     0x20 /* CIF format */
#define COM7_FMT_QVGA    0x10 /* QVGA format */
#define COM7_FMT_QCIF    0x08 /* QCIF format */
#define COM7_RGB       0x04 /* bits 0 and 2 - RGB for-
mat */
#define COM7_YUV     0x00 /* YUV */
#define COM7_BAYER     0x01 /* Bayer format */
#define COM7_PBAYER     0x05 /* "Processed bayer"
*/
#define REG_COM8  0x13 /* Control 8 */
#define COM8_FASTAEC     0x80 /* Enable fast AGC/
AEC */
#define COM8_AECSTEP      0x40 /* Unlimited AEC
```

```
step size */
#define COM8_BFILT   0x20 /* Band filter enable */
#define COM8_AGC   0x04 /* Auto gain enable */
#define COM8_AWB   0x02 /* White balance enable */
#define COM8_AEC   0x01 /* Auto exposure enable */
#define REG_COM9   0x14 /* Control 9- gain ceiling */
#define REG_COM10  0x15 /* Control 10 */
#define COM10_HSYNC      0x40 /* HSYNC instead of
HREF */
#define COM10_PCLK_HB      0x20 /* Suppress PCLK
on horiz blank */
#define COM10_HREF_REV      0x08 /* Reverse HREF
*/
#define COM10_VS_LEAD      0x04 /* VSYNC on clock
leading edge */
#define COM10_VS_NEG      0x02 /* VSYNC negative
*/
#define COM10_HS_NEG      0x01 /* HSYNC negative
*/
#define REG_HSTART   0x17 /* Horiz start high bits */
#define REG_HSTOP  0x18 /* Horiz stop high bits */
#define REG_VSTART   0x19 /* Vert start high bits */
#define REG_VSTOP  0x1a /* Vert stop high bits */
#define REG_PSHFT  0x1b /* Pixel delay after HREF */
#define REG_MIDH   0x1c /* Manuf. ID high */
#define REG_MIDL   0x1d /* Manuf. ID low */
#define REG_MVFP   0x1e /* Mirror / vflip */
#define MVFP_MIRROR      0x20 /* Mirror image */
#define MVFP_FLIP  0x10 /* Vertical flip */
#define REG_AEW      0x24 /* AGC upper limit */
#define REG_AEB      0x25 /* AGC lower limit */
```

```
#define REG_VPT        0x26  /* AGC/AEC fast mode op region */
#define REG_HSYST  0x30  /* HSYNC rising edge delay */
#define REG_HSYEN  0x31  /* HSYNC falling edge delay */
#define REG_HREF   0x32  /* HREF pieces */
#define REG_TSLB   0x3a  /* lots of stuff */
#define TSLB_YLAST    0x04  /* UYVY or VYUY - see com13 */
#define REG_COM11 0x3b  /* Control 11 */
#define COM11_NIGHT    0x80  /* NIght mode enable */
#define COM11_NMFR     0x60  /* Two bit NM frame rate */
#define COM11_HZAUTO       0x10  /* Auto detect 50/60 Hz */
#define COM11_50HZ    0x08  /* Manual 50Hz select */
#define COM11_EXP 0x02
#define REG_COM12 0x3c  /* Control 12 */
#define COM12_HREF     0x80  /* HREF always */
#define REG_COM13 0x3d  /* Control 13 */
#define COM13_GAMMA    0x80  /* Gamma enable */
#define COM13_UVSAT    0x40  /* UV saturation auto adjustment */
#define COM13_UVSWAP       0x01  /* V before U - w/ TSLB */
#define REG_COM14 0x3e  /* Control 14 */
#define COM14_DCWEN    0x10  /* DCW/PCLK-scale enable */
```

```
#define REG_EDGE   0x3f /* Edge enhancement factor
*/
#define REG_COM15  0x40 /* Control 15 */
#define COM15_R10F0      0x00 /* Data range 10 to F0
*/
#define COM15_R01FE      0x80 /*   01 to FE */
#define COM15_R00FF      0xc0 /*   00 to FF */
#define COM15_RGB565     0x10 /* RGB565 output */
#define COM15_RGB555     0x30 /* RGB555 output */
#define REG_COM16  0x41 /* Control 16 */
#define COM16_AWBGAIN      0x08 /* AWB gain en-
able */
#define REG_COM17  0x42 /* Control 17 */
#define COM17_AECWIN       0xc0 /* AEC window -
must match COM4 */
#define COM17_CBAR    0x08 /* DSP Color bar */
/*
* This matrix defines how the colors are generated,
must be
* tweaked to adjust hue and saturation.
*
* Order: v-red, v-green, v-blue, u-red, u-green, u-blue
* They are nine-bit signed quantities, with the sign bit
* stored in0x58.Sign for v-red is bit 0, and up from
there.
*/
#define REG_CMATRIX_BASE 0x4f
#define CMATRIX_LEN      6
#define REG_CMATRIX_SIGN 0x58
#define REG_BRIGHT   0x55 /* Brightness */
#define REG_CONTRAS    0x56 /* Contrast control */
```

```
#define REG_GFIX   0x69 /* Fix gain control */
#define REG_REG76  0x76 /* OV's name */
#define R76_BLKPCOR    0x80 /* Black pixel correction enable */
#define R76_WHTPCOR     0x40 /* White pixel correction enable */
#define REG_RGB444     0x8c /* RGB 444 control */
#define R444_ENABLE     0x02 /* Turn on RGB444, overrides 5x5 */
#define R444_RGBX 0x01 /* Empty nibble at end */
#define REG_HAECC1  0x9f /* Hist AEC/AGC control 1 */
#define REG_HAECC2 0xa0 /* Hist AEC/AGC control 2 */
#define REG_BD50MAX    0xa5 /* 50hz banding step limit */
#define REG_HAECC3  0xa6 /* Hist AEC/AGC control 3 */
#define REG_HAECC4  0xa7 /* Hist AEC/AGC control 4 */
#define REG_HAECC5  0xa8 /* Hist AEC/AGC control 5 */
#define REG_HAECC6  0xa9 /* Hist AEC/AGC control 6 */
#define REG_HAECC7  0xaa /* Hist AEC/AGC control 7 */
#define REG_BD60MAX    0xab /* 60hz banding step limit */
#define REG_GAIN   0x00 /* Gain lower 8 bits (rest in vref) */
#define REG_BLUE   0x01 /* blue gain */
```

```
#define REG_RED      0x02 /* red gain */
#define REG_VREF     0x03 /* Pieces of GAIN, VSTART, VSTOP */
#define REG_COM1     0x04 /* Control 1 */
#define COM1_CCIR656     0x40 /* CCIR656 enable */
#define REG_BAVE     0x05 /* U/B Average level */
#define REG_GbAVE    0x06 /* Y/Gb Average level */
#define REG_AECHH    0x07 /* AEC MS 5 bits */
#define REG_RAVE     0x08 /* V/R Average level */
#define REG_COM2     0x09 /* Control 2 */
#define COM2_SSLEEP      0x10 /* Soft sleep mode */
#define REG_PID      0x0a /* Product ID MSB */
#define REG_VER      0x0b /* Product ID LSB */
#define REG_COM3     0x0c /* Control 3 */
#define COM3_SWAP        0x40 /* Byte swap */
#define COM3_SCALEEN     0x08 /* Enable scaling */
#define COM3_DCWEN       0x04 /* Enable downsamp/crop/window */
#define REG_COM4     0x0d /* Control 4 */
#define REG_COM5     0x0e /* All "reserved" */
#define REG_COM6     0x0f /* Control 6 */
#define REG_AECH     0x10 /* More bits of AEC value */
#define REG_CLKRC    0x11 /* Clocl control */
#define CLK_EXT      0x40 /* Use external clock directly */
#define CLK_SCALE    0x3f /* Mask for internal clock scale */
#define REG_COM7     0x12 /* Control 7 */
#define COM7_RESET       0x80 /* Register reset */
#define COM7_FMT_MASK    0x38
#define COM7_FMT_VGA     0x00
```

```
#define COM7_FMT_CIF      0x20 /* CIF format */
#define COM7_FMT_QVGA     0x10 /* QVGA format */
#define COM7_FMT_QCIF     0x08 /* QCIF format */
#define COM7_RGB   0x04 /* bits 0 and 2 - RGB format */
#define COM7_YUV   0x00 /* YUV */
#define COM7_BAYER       0x01 /* Bayer format */
#define COM7_PBAYER      0x05 /* "Processed bayer" */
#define REG_COM8  0x13 /* Control 8 */
#define COM8_FASTAEC      0x80 /* Enable fast AGC/AEC */
#define COM8_AECSTEP      0x40 /* Unlimited AEC step size */
#define COM8_BFILT   0x20 /* Band filter enable */
#define COM8_AGC   0x04 /* Auto gain enable */
#define COM8_AWB   0x02 /* White balance enable */
#define COM8_AEC   0x01 /* Auto exposure enable */
#define REG_COM9   0x14 /* Control 9- gain ceiling */
#define REG_COM10  0x15 /* Control 10 */
#define COM10_HSYNC      0x40 /* HSYNC instead of HREF */
#define COM10_PCLK_HB     0x20 /* Suppress PCLK on horiz blank */
#define COM10_HREF_REV     0x08 /* Reverse HREF */
#define COM10_VS_LEAD     0x04 /* VSYNC on clock leading edge */
#define COM10_VS_NEG      0x02 /* VSYNC negative */
#define COM10_HS_NEG      0x01 /* HSYNC negative
```

```
*/
#define REG_HSTART   0x17 /* Horiz start high bits */
#define REG_HSTOP  0x18 /* Horiz stop high bits */
#define REG_VSTART   0x19 /* Vert start high bits */
#define REG_VSTOP  0x1a /* Vert stop high bits */
#define REG_PSHFT  0x1b /* Pixel delay after HREF */
#define REG_MIDH   0x1c /* Manuf. ID high */
#define REG_MIDL   0x1d /* Manuf. ID low */
#define REG_MVFP   0x1e /* Mirror / vflip */
#define MVFP_MIRROR     0x20 /* Mirror image */
#define MVFP_FLIP  0x10 /* Vertical flip */
#define REG_AEW      0x24 /* AGC upper limit */
#define REG_AEB      0x25 /* AGC lower limit */
#define REG_VPT       0x26 /* AGC/AEC fast mode op
region */
#define REG_HSYST  0x30 /* HSYNC rising edge delay
*/
#define REG_HSYEN  0x31 /* HSYNC falling edge de-
lay */
#define REG_HREF   0x32 /* HREF pieces */
#define REG_TSLB   0x3a /* lots of stuff */
#define TSLB_YLAST   0x04  /* UYVY or VYUY - see
com13 */
#define REG_COM11 0x3b /* Control 11 */
#define COM11_NIGHT     0x80 /* NIght mode enable
*/
#define COM11_NMFR      0x60 /* Two bit NM frame
rate */
#define COM11_HZAUTO       0x10  /* Auto detect
50/60 Hz */
#define COM11_50HZ      0x08 /* Manual 50Hz select
```

```
*/
#define COM11_EXP  0x02
#define REG_COM12 0x3c /* Control 12 */
#define COM12_HREF     0x80 /* HREF always */
#define REG_COM13 0x3d /* Control 13 */
#define COM13_GAMMA     0x80 /* Gamma enable */
#define COM13_UVSAT     0x40 /* UV saturation auto
adjustment */
#define COM13_UVSWAP     0x01 /* V before U - w/
TSLB */
#define REG_COM14 0x3e /* Control 14 */
#define COM14_DCWEN     0x10 /* DCW/PCLK-scale
enable */
#define REG_EDGE  0x3f /* Edge enhancement factor
*/
#define REG_COM15 0x40 /* Control 15 */
#define COM15_R10F0     0x00 /* Data range 10 to F0
*/
#define COM15_R01FE     0x80 /*   01 to FE */
#define COM15_R00FF     0xc0 /*   00 to FF */
#define COM15_RGB565     0x10 /* RGB565 output */
#define COM15_RGB555     0x30 /* RGB555 output */
#define REG_COM16 0x41 /* Control 16 */
#define COM16_AWBGAIN     0x08 /* AWB gain en-
able */
#define REG_COM17 0x42 /* Control 17 */
#define COM17_AECWIN     0xc0 /* AEC window -
must match COM4 */
#define COM17_CBAR     0x08 /* DSP Color bar */
#define CMATRIX_LEN     6
#define REG_BRIGHT 0x55 /* Brightness */
```

```
#define REG_REG76  0x76 /* OV's name */
#define R76_BLKPCOR      0x80 /* Black pixel correc-
tion enable */
#define R76_WHTPCOR       0x40 /* White pixel cor-
rection enable */
#define REG_RGB444      0x8c /* RGB 444 control */
#define R444_ENABLE      0x02 /* Turn on RGB444,
overrides 5x5 */
#define R444_RGBX  0x01 /* Empty nibble at end */
#define REG_HAECC1  0x9f /* Hist AEC/AGC control 1
*/
#define REG_HAECC2  0xa0 /* Hist AEC/AGC control
2 */
#define REG_BD50MAX     0xa5 /* 50hz banding step
limit */
#define REG_HAECC3  0xa6 /* Hist AEC/AGC control
3 */
#define REG_HAECC4  0xa7 /* Hist AEC/AGC control
4 */
#define REG_HAECC5  0xa8 /* Hist AEC/AGC control
5 */
#define REG_HAECC6  0xa9 /* Hist AEC/AGC control
6 */
#define REG_HAECC7  0xaa /* Hist AEC/AGC control
7 */
#define REG_BD60MAX     0xab /* 60hz banding step
limit */
#define MTX1       0x4f /* Matrix Coefficient 1 */
#define MTX2       0x50 /* Matrix Coefficient 2 */
#define MTX3       0x51 /* Matrix Coefficient 3 */
#define MTX4       0x52 /* Matrix Coefficient 4 */
```

```
#define MTX5       0x53 /* Matrix Coefficient 5 */
#define MTX6       0x54 /* Matrix Coefficient 6 */
#define REG_CONTRAS    0x56 /* Contrast control */
#define MTXS       0x58 /* Matrix Coefficient Sign */
#define AWBC7      0x59 /* AWB Control 7 */
#define AWBC8      0x5a /* AWB Control 8 */
#define AWBC9      0x5b /* AWB Control 9 */
#define AWBC10     0x5c /* AWB Control 10 */
#define AWBC11     0x5d /* AWB Control 11 */
#define AWBC12     0x5e /* AWB Control 12 */
#define REG_GFI    0x69 /* Fix gain control */
#define GGAIN      0x6a /* G Channel AWB Gain */
#define DBLV       0x6b
#define AWBCTR3    0x6c /* AWB Control 3 */
#define AWBCTR2    0x6d /* AWB Control 2 */
#define AWBCTR1    0x6e /* AWB Control 1 */
#define AWBCTR0    0x6f /* AWB Control 0 */
struct regval_list{
 uint8_t reg_num;
 uint16_t value;
};
const struct regval_list qvga_ov7670[] PROGMEM = {
 { REG_COM14, 0x19 },
 { 0x72, 0x11 },
 { 0x73, 0xf1 },
  { REG_HSTART, 0x16 },
 { REG_HSTOP, 0x04 },
 { REG_HREF, 0xa4 },
 { REG_VSTART, 0x02 },
 { REG_VSTOP, 0x7a },
```

```
{ REG_VREF, 0x0a },
  { 0xff, 0xff }, /* END MARKER */
};
const struct regval_list yuv422_ov7670[] PROGMEM
= {
 { REG_COM7, 0x0 }, /* Selects YUV mode */
 { REG_RGB444, 0 }, /* No RGB444 please */
 { REG_COM1, 0 },
 { REG_COM15, COM15_R00FF },
  { REG_COM9, 0x6A }, /* 128x gain ceiling; 0x8 is re-
served bit */
 { 0x4f, 0x80 }, /* "matrix coefficient 1" */
 { 0x50, 0x80 },  /* "matrix coefficient 2" */
 { 0x51, 0 },  /* vb */
 { 0x52, 0x22 }, /* "matrix coefficient 4" */
 { 0x53, 0x5e },  /* "matrix coefficient 5" */
 { 0x54, 0x80 },  /* "matrix coefficient 6" */
 { REG_COM13, COM13_UVSAT },
 { 0xff, 0xff },  /* END MARKER */
};
const struct regval_list ov7670_default_regs[] PROG-
MEM = {//from the linux driver
 { REG_COM7, COM7_RESET },
 { REG_TSLB, 0x04 }, /* OV */
 { REG_COM7, 0 }, /* VGA */
 /*
 * Set the hardware window.  These values from OV
don't entirely
 * make sense - hstop is less than hstart.  But they
work...
```

```
*/
{ REG_HSTART, 0x13 }, { REG_HSTOP, 0x01 },
{ REG_HREF, 0xb6 }, { REG_VSTART, 0x02 },
{ REG_VSTOP, 0x7a }, { REG_VREF, 0x0a },
 { REG_COM3, 0 }, { REG_COM14, 0 },
/* Mystery scaling numbers */
{ 0x70, 0x3a }, { 0x71, 0x35 },
{ 0x72, 0x11 }, { 0x73, 0xf0 },
{ 0xa2,/* 0x02 changed to 1*/1 }, { REG_COM10, 0x0 },
/* Gamma curve values */
{ 0x7a, 0x20 }, { 0x7b, 0x10 },
{ 0x7c, 0x1e }, { 0x7d, 0x35 },
{ 0x7e, 0x5a }, { 0x7f, 0x69 },
{ 0x80, 0x76 }, { 0x81, 0x80 },
{ 0x82, 0x88 }, { 0x83, 0x8f },
{ 0x84, 0x96 }, { 0x85, 0xa3 },
{ 0x86, 0xaf }, { 0x87, 0xc4 },
{ 0x88, 0xd7 }, { 0x89, 0xe8 },
 /* AGC and AEC parameters.  Note we start by disab-
ling those features,
then turn them only after tweaking the values. */
{ REG_COM8, COM8_FASTAEC | COM8_AECSTEP },
{ REG_GAIN, 0 }, { REG_AECH, 0 },
{ REG_COM4, 0x40 }, /* magic reserved bit */
{ REG_COM9, 0x18 }, /* 4x gain + magic rsvd bit */
{ REG_BD50MAX, 0x05 }, { REG_BD60MAX, 0x07 },
{ REG_AEW, 0x95 }, { REG_AEB, 0x33 },
{ REG_VPT, 0xe3 }, { REG_HAECC1, 0x78 },
{ REG_HAECC2, 0x68 }, { 0xa1, 0x03 }, /* magic */
{ REG_HAECC3, 0xd8 }, { REG_HAECC4, 0xd8 },
{ REG_HAECC5, 0xf0 }, { REG_HAECC6, 0x90 },
```

```
{ REG_HAECC7, 0x94 },
  { REG_COM8, COM8_FASTAEC | COM8_AECSTEP |
COM8_AGC | COM8_AEC },
{ 0x30, 0 }, { 0x31, 0 },//disable some delays
/* Almost all of these are magic "reserved" values. */
{ REG_COM5, 0x61 }, { REG_COM6, 0x4b },
{ 0x16, 0x02 }, { REG_MVFP, 0x07 },
{ 0x21, 0x02 }, { 0x22, 0x91 },
{ 0x29, 0x07 }, { 0x33, 0x0b },
{ 0x35, 0x0b }, { 0x37, 0x1d },
{ 0x38, 0x71 }, { 0x39, 0x2a },
{ REG_COM12, 0x78 }, { 0x4d, 0x40 },
{ 0x4e, 0x20 }, { REG_GFIX, 0 },
/*{0x6b, 0x4a},*/{ 0x74, 0x10 },
{ 0x8d, 0x4f }, { 0x8e, 0 },
{ 0x8f, 0 }, { 0x90, 0 },
{ 0x91, 0 }, { 0x96, 0 },
{ 0x9a, 0 }, { 0xb0, 0x84 },
{ 0xb1, 0x0c }, { 0xb2, 0x0e },
{ 0xb3, 0x82 }, { 0xb8, 0x0a },

  /* More reserved magic, some of which tweaks white
balance */
{ 0x43, 0x0a }, { 0x44, 0xf0 },
{ 0x45, 0x34 }, { 0x46, 0x58 },
{ 0x47, 0x28 }, { 0x48, 0x3a },
{ 0x59, 0x88 }, { 0x5a, 0x88 },
{ 0x5b, 0x44 }, { 0x5c, 0x67 },
{ 0x5d, 0x49 }, { 0x5e, 0x0e },
{ 0x6c, 0x0a }, { 0x6d, 0x55 },
{ 0x6e, 0x11 }, { 0x6f, 0x9e }, /* it was 0x9F "9e for ad-
vance AWB" */
```

```
{ 0x6a, 0x40 }, { REG_BLUE, 0x40 },
{ REG_RED, 0x60 },
  { REG_COM8, COM8_FASTAEC | COM8_AECSTEP |
COM8_AGC | COM8_AEC | COM8_AWB },
  /* Matrix coefficients */
{ 0x4f, 0x80 }, { 0x50, 0x80 },
{ 0x51, 0 },  { 0x52, 0x22 },
{ 0x53, 0x5e }, { 0x54, 0x80 },
{ 0x58, 0x9e },
  { REG_COM16, COM16_AWBGAIN }, { REG_EDGE, 0 },
{ 0x75, 0x05 }, { REG_REG76, 0xe1 },
{ 0x4c, 0 },  { 0x77, 0x01 },
{ REG_COM13, /*0xc3*/0x48 }, { 0x4b, 0x09 },
{ 0xc9, 0x60 },  /*{REG_COM16, 0x38},*/
{ 0x56, 0x40 },
  { 0x34, 0x11 }, { REG_COM11, COM11_EXP |
COM11_HZAUTO },
{ 0xa4, 0x82/*Was 0x88*/ }, { 0x96, 0 },
{ 0x97, 0x30 }, { 0x98, 0x20 },
{ 0x99, 0x30 }, { 0x9a, 0x84 },
{ 0x9b, 0x29 }, { 0x9c, 0x03 },
{ 0x9d, 0x4c }, { 0x9e, 0x3f },
{ 0x78, 0x04 },
  /* Extra-weird stuff. Some sort of multiplexor regis-
ter */
{ 0x79, 0x01 }, { 0xc8, 0xf0 },
{ 0x79, 0x0f }, { 0xc8, 0x00 },
{ 0x79, 0x10 }, { 0xc8, 0x7e },
{ 0x79, 0x0a }, { 0xc8, 0x80 },
{ 0x79, 0x0b }, { 0xc8, 0x01 },
```

```
    { 0x79, 0x0c }, { 0xc8, 0x0f },
    { 0x79, 0x0d }, { 0xc8, 0x20 },
    { 0x79, 0x09 }, { 0xc8, 0x80 },
    { 0x79, 0x02 }, { 0xc8, 0xc0 },
    { 0x79, 0x03 }, { 0xc8, 0x40 },
    { 0x79, 0x05 }, { 0xc8, 0x30 },
    { 0x79, 0x26 },
    { 0xff, 0xff }, /* END MARKER */
};
void error_led(void){
 DDRB |= 32;//make sure led is output
 while (1){//wait for reset
  PORTB ^= 32;// toggle led
  _delay_ms(100);
 }
}
void twiStart(void){
 TWCR = _BV(TWINT) | _BV(TWSTA) | _BV(TWEN);//
send start
  while (!(TWCR & (1 << TWINT)));//wait for start to
be transmitted
 if ((TWSR & 0xF8) != TW_START)
  error_led();
}
void twiWriteByte(uint8_t DATA, uint8_t type){
 TWDR = DATA;
 TWCR = _BV(TWINT) | _BV(TWEN);
 while (!(TWCR & (1 << TWINT))) {}
 if ((TWSR & 0xF8) != type)
  error_led();
```

```
}
void twiAddr(uint8_t addr, uint8_t typeTWI){
 TWDR = addr;//send address
 TWCR = _BV(TWINT) | _BV(TWEN);    /* clear inter-
rupt to start transmission */
 while ((TWCR & _BV(TWINT)) == 0); /* wait for trans-
mission */
 if ((TWSR & 0xF8) != typeTWI)
  error_led();
}
voidwriteReg(uint8_t reg, uint8_t dat){
 //send start condition
 twiStart();
 twiAddr(camAddr_WR, TW_MT_SLA_ACK);
 twiWriteByte(reg, TW_MT_DATA_ACK);
 twiWriteByte(dat, TW_MT_DATA_ACK);
   TWCR = (1 << TWINT) | (1 << TWEN) | (1 <<
TWSTO);//send stop
 _delay_ms(1);
}
static uint8_t twiRd(uint8_t nack){
 if(nack){
  TWCR = _BV(TWINT) | _BV(TWEN);
   while ((TWCR & _BV(TWINT)) == 0); /* wait for
transmission */
  if ((TWSR & 0xF8) != TW_MR_DATA_NACK)
   error_led();
  return TWDR;
 }
 else{
```

```
 TWCR = _BV(TWINT) | _BV(TWEN) | _BV(TWEA);
   while ((TWCR & _BV(TWINT)) == 0); /* wait for
transmission */
  if ((TWSR & 0xF8) != TW_MR_DATA_ACK)
   error_led();
  return TWDR;
 }
}
uint8_t rdReg(uint8_t reg){
 uint8_t dat;
 twiStart();
 twiAddr(camAddr_WR, TW_MT_SLA_ACK);
 twiWriteByte(reg, TW_MT_DATA_ACK);
   TWCR = (1 << TWINT) | (1 << TWEN) | (1 <<
TWSTO);//send stop
 _delay_ms(1);
 twiStart();
 twiAddr(camAddr_RD, TW_MR_SLA_ACK);
 dat = twiRd(1);
   TWCR = (1 << TWINT) | (1 << TWEN) | (1 <<
TWSTO);//send stop
 _delay_ms(1);
 return dat;
}
void wrSensorRegs8_8(const struct regval_list reg-
list[]){
 uint8_t reg_addr, reg_val;
 const struct regval_list *next = reglist;
 while ((reg_addr != 0xff) | (reg_val != 0xff)){
  reg_addr = pgm_read_byte(&next->reg_num);
```

```
  reg_val = pgm_read_byte(&next->value);
  writeReg(reg_addr, reg_val);
  next++;
 }
}
void setColor(void){
 wrSensorRegs8_8(yuv422_ov7670);
// wrSensorRegs8_8(qvga_ov7670);
}
void setResolution(void){
 writeReg(REG_COM3, 4); // REG_COM3 enable scal-
ing
 wrSensorRegs8_8(qvga_ov7670);
}
void camInit(void){
writeReg(0x12, 0x80);
 _delay_ms(100);
 wrSensorRegs8_8(ov7670_default_regs);
 writeReg(REG_COM10, 32);//PCLK does not toggle
on HBLANK.
}
void arduinoUnoInut(void) {
 cli();//disable interrupts


   /* Setup the 8mhz PWM clock
  * This will be on pin 11*/
 DDRB |= (1 << 3);//pin 11
 ASSR &= ~(_BV(EXCLK) | _BV(AS2));
  TCCR2A = (1 << COM2A0) | (1 << WGM21) | (1 <<
```

```
WGM20);
 TCCR2B = (1 << WGM22) | (1 << CS20);
 OCR2A = 0;//(F_CPU)/(2*(X+1))
 DDRC &= ~15;//low d0-d3 camera
 DDRD &= ~252;//d7-d4 and interrupt pins
 _delay_ms(3000);


   //set up twi for 100khz
 TWSR &= ~3;//disable prescaler for TWI
 TWBR = 72;//set to 100khz


   //enable serial
 UBRR0H = 0;
 UBRR0L = 1;//0 = 2M baud rate. 1 = 1M baud. 3 = 0.5M.
7 = 250k 207 is 9600 baud rate.
 UCSR0A |= 2;//double speed aysnc
 UCSR0B = (1 << RXEN0) | (1 << TXEN0);//Enable re-
ceiver and transmitter
 UCSR0C = 6;//async 1 stop bit 8bit char no parity bits
}
void StringPgm(const char * str){
 do{
   while (!(UCSR0A & (1 << UDRE0)));//wait for byte to
transmit
   UDR0 = pgm_read_byte_near(str);
   while (!(UCSR0A & (1 << UDRE0)));//wait for byte to
transmit
 } while (pgm_read_byte_near(++str));
}
```

```
static void captureImg(uint16_t wg, uint16_t hg){
 uint16_t y, x;
  StringPgm(PSTR("*RDY*"));
  while (!(PIND & 8));//wait for high
 while ((PIND & 8));//wait for low
    y = hg;
 while (y--){
   x = wg;
  //while (!(PIND & 256));//wait for high
  while (x--){
   while ((PIND & 4));//wait for low
     UDR0 = (PINC & 15) | (PIND & 240);
     while (!(UCSR0A & (1 << UDRE0)));//wait for byte
to transmit
   while (!(PIND & 4));//wait for high
   while ((PIND & 4));//wait for low
   while (!(PIND & 4));//wait for high
  }
  // while ((PIND & 256));//wait for low
 }
  _delay_ms(100);
}
void setup(){
 arduinoUnoInut();
 camInit();
 setResolution();
 setColor();
  writeReg(0x11, 10); //Earlier it had the value:
writeReg(0x11, 12); New version works better for
me :) !!!!
```

```
}
void loop(){
 captureImg(320, 240);
}
```

9.OBSTACLE AVOIDING ROBOT USING ARDUINO AND ULTRASONIC SENSOR

Impediment Avoiding Robot is a smart gadget which can naturally detect the snag before it and keep away from them by turning itself toward another path. This plan enables the robot to explore in obscure condition by maintaining a strategic distance from impacts, which is an essential prerequisite for any self-sufficient portable robot. The use of Obstacle Avoiding robot isn't restricted and it is utilized in a large portion of the military association now which helps do numerous hazardous employments that is impossible by any troopers.

We recently constructed Obstacle Avoiding Robot utilizing Raspberry Pi and utilizing PIC Microcontroller. This time we utilize Arduino as well as Ultrasonic Sensor to assemble an Obstacle Avoider. Here a Ultrasonic sensor is utilized to detect the deterrents in the way by figuring the separation between the robot and obstruction. In the event that robot finds any impediment it alters the course and keep moving.

How Ultrasonic Sensor can be used to Avoid Obstacles

Prior to going to manufacture the robot, it is essential to see how the ultrasonic sensor functions since this sensor will have significant job in distinguishing impediment. The fundamental standard behind the working of ultrasonic sensor is to note down the time taken by sensor to transmit ultrasonic bars and getting the ultrasonic bars subsequent to hitting the surface. At that point further the separation is determined utilizing the recipe. In this task, the generally accessible HC-SR04 Ultrasonic Sensor is utilized. To utilize this sensor, comparable methodology will be pursued clarified previously.

Thus, the Trig stick of HC-SR04 is made high for in any event 10 us. A sonic pillar is transmitted with 8 heart-beats of 40KHz each.

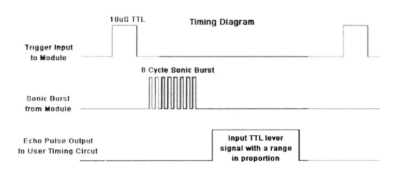

The sign at that point hits the surface and return back and caught by the beneficiary Echo stick of HC-SR04. The Echo stick had officially made high at the time sending high.

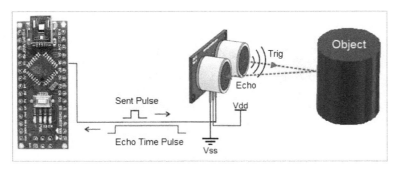

The time taken by bar to return back is spared in factor and changed over to separation utilizing suitable computations like beneath

Distance= (Time x Speed of Sound in Air (343 m/s))/2

We utilized ultrasonic sensor in numerous ventures, to get familiar with Ultrasonic sensor, check different activities identified with Ultrasonic sensor.

The parts for this hindrance keeping away from robot can be found effectively. So as to make skeleton, any toy case can be utilized or can be uniquely crafted.

Components Required

1. Arduino NANO or Uno (any version)
2. 5V DC Motors
3. Wheels
4. LM298N Motor Driver Module

5. Battery
6. Jumper Wires
7. Chassis
8. HC-SR04 Ultrasonic Sensor

Circuit Diagram

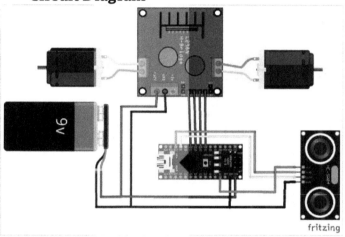

Programming Arduino for Obstacle Avoiding Robot

Complete program is given toward the part of the bargain. The program will incorporate setting up HC-SR04 module and yielding the sign to Motor Pins to move engine bearing in like manner. No libraries will be utilized in this venture.

First characterize trig and reverberation stick of HC-SR04 in the program. In this venture the trig stick is associated with GPIO9 and reverberation stick is associated with GPIO 10 of Arduino NANO.

```
int trigPin = 9;   // trig pin of HC-SR04

int echoPin = 10;   // Echo pin of HC-SR04
```

Characterize pins for contribution of LM298N Motor Driver Module. The LM298N has 4 information info pins used to control the heading of engine associated with it.

```
int revleft4 = 4;    //REVerse motion of Left motor

int fwdleft5 = 5;       //ForWarD motion of Left
motor

int revright6 = 6;      //REVerse motion of Right
motor

int fwdright7 = 7;      //ForWarD motion of Right
motor
```

Anbazhagan k

In arrangement() work, characterize the information bearing of used GPIO pins. The four Motor pins and Trig stick is set as OUTPUT as well as Echo Pin is set as Input.

pinMode(revleft4, OUTPUT);   // set Motor pins as output

pinMode(fwdleft5, OUTPUT);

pinMode(revright6, OUTPUT);

pinMode(fwdright7, OUTPUT);

pinMode(trigPin, OUTPUT);   // set trig pin as output

pinMode(echoPin, INPUT);   //set echo pin as

input to capture reflected waves

In circle() work, get the good ways from HC-SR04 and dependent on the separation move the engine course. The separation will demonstrate the article separation coming before the robot. The Distance is taken by blasting a light emission up to 10 us and getting it after 10us. To get familiar with estimating separation utilizing Ultrasonic sensor and Arduino, pursue the connection.

```
digitalWrite(trigPin, LOW);

delayMicroseconds(2);

digitalWrite(trigPin, HIGH);   // send waves for 10 us

delayMicroseconds(10);

duration = pulseIn(echoPin, HIGH); // receive reflected waves

distance = duration / 58.2;  // convert to distance

delay(10);
```

In case the separation is more noteworthy than the characterized separation implies there isn't hindrance in its way and it will moving forward way.

```
if (distance > 19)

    {

    digitalWrite(fwdright7, HIGH);          //
move forward

    digitalWrite(revright6, LOW);

    digitalWrite(fwdleft5, HIGH);

    digitalWrite(revleft4, LOW);

    }
```

In case the separation is not exactly the characterized separation to keep away from obstruction implies there is some hindrance ahead. So in this circumstance robot will stop for some time and moveback-wards after that again stop for some time and after-ward take go to another course.

```
if (distance < 18)

    {

    digitalWrite(fwdright7, LOW); //Stop
```

```
digitalWrite(revright6, LOW);

digitalWrite(fwdleft5, LOW);

digitalWrite(revleft4, LOW);

delay(500);

digitalWrite(fwdright7, LOW);    //move-
backword

digitalWrite(revright6, HIGH);

digitalWrite(fwdleft5, LOW);

digitalWrite(revleft4, HIGH);

delay(500);

digitalWrite(fwdright7, LOW); //Stop

digitalWrite(revright6, LOW);

digitalWrite(fwdleft5, LOW);

digitalWrite(revleft4, LOW);

delay(100);

digitalWrite(fwdright7, HIGH);
```

```
    digitalWrite(revright6, LOW);

    digitalWrite(revleft4, LOW);

    digitalWrite(fwdleft5, LOW);

    delay(500);

}
```

So this is the way a robot can maintain a tactical distance from snags in its way without stalling out anyplace.

Code

/* Obstacle Avoiding Robot Using Ultrasonic Sensor and Arduino NANO

*/
```
int trigPin = 9;   // trig pin of HC-SR04
int echoPin = 10;   // Echo pin of HC-SR04
int revleft4 = 4;    //REVerse motion of Left motor
int fwdleft5 = 5;    //ForWarD motion of Left motor
int revright6 = 6;   //REVerse motion of Right motor
int fwdright7 = 7;   //ForWarD motion of Right motor
long duration, distance;
void setup() {
```

```
  delay(random(500,2000));    // delay for random
time
  Serial.begin(9600);
  pinMode(revleft4, OUTPUT);    // set Motor pins as
output
  pinMode(fwdleft5, OUTPUT);
  pinMode(revright6, OUTPUT);
  pinMode(fwdright7, OUTPUT);


  pinMode(trigPin, OUTPUT);        // set trig pin as
output
  pinMode(echoPin, INPUT);      //set echo pin as input
to capture reflected waves
}
void loop() {
  digitalWrite(trigPin, LOW);
  delayMicroseconds(2);
  digitalWrite(trigPin, HIGH);   // send waves for 10 us
  delayMicroseconds(10);
  duration = pulseIn(echoPin, HIGH); // receive re-
flected waves
  distance = duration / 58.2; // convert to distance
  delay(10);
  // If you dont get proper movements of your robot
then alter the pin numbers
  if(distance > 19)
  {
    digitalWrite(fwdright7, HIGH);             // move
forward
```

```
  digitalWrite(revright6, LOW);
  digitalWrite(fwdleft5, HIGH);
  digitalWrite(revleft4, LOW);
}
  if(distance < 18)
{
  digitalWrite(fwdright7, LOW); //Stop
  digitalWrite(revright6, LOW);
  digitalWrite(fwdleft5, LOW);
  digitalWrite(revleft4, LOW);
  delay(500);
  digitalWrite(fwdright7, LOW);    //movebackword

  digitalWrite(revright6, HIGH);
  digitalWrite(fwdleft5, LOW);
  digitalWrite(revleft4, HIGH);
  delay(500);
  digitalWrite(fwdright7, LOW); //Stop
  digitalWrite(revright6, LOW);
  digitalWrite(fwdleft5, LOW);
  digitalWrite(revleft4, LOW);
  delay(100);
  digitalWrite(fwdright7, HIGH);
  digitalWrite(revright6, LOW);
  digitalWrite(revleft4, LOW);
  digitalWrite(fwdleft5, LOW);
  delay(500);
}
}
```

10. 7.4V TWO STEP LITHIUM BATTERY CHARGER CIRCUIT - CC AND CV MODE

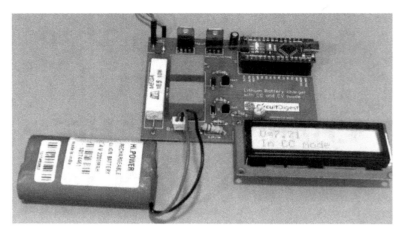

The progression in Electric Vehicles, Drone and other versatile hardware like IoT Devices is by all accounts promising for what's to come. One normal thing among all these is that they are altogether fueled by batteries. Following Moore's law the electronic gadgets will in general become littler and progressively consumable, these versatile gadgets ought to have their very own wellspring of capacity to work. The most widely recognized battery decision for compact gadgets today is Lithium Ion or Lithium Polymer Batteries. While these Batteries have an awesome charge thickness they are artificially shaky under unforgiving conditions thus care ought to be taken while charging them and utilizing them.

In this venture we will assemble a Two Stage Battery charger (CC and CV) that could be utilized as to charge Lithium particle or lithium polymer players. The battery charger circuit is intended for 7.4V lithium battery pack (two 18650 in Series) which I regularly use in many mechanical technology venture yet the circuit can be effectively altered to fit in lower or somewhat higher battery Packs like to fabricate 3.7 lithium battery charger or 12v lithium particle battery Charger. You may know there are instant Chargers accessible for these batteries, however those that are modest are moderate and those that are quick are over the top expensive. So in this circuit I chose to manufacture a straightforward rough charger with LM317 ICs with CC and CV mode. Additionally, what's better time than structure your very own contraption and learning in it's procedure.

Keep in mind that Lithium batteries ought to be dealt with cautiously. Cheating it or Shorting it may prompt blast and fire peril, so remain safe around it. In case you are totally new to lithium batteries, at that point I would unequivocally encourage you to peruse the Lithium battery article, before continuing further. That being said we should get into the undertaking.

CC and CV mode for Battery Charger:

The Charger that we expectation to work here is a Two Step Charger, which means it will have two charging modes to be specific Constant Charge (CC) and Constant Voltage (CV). By consolidating these two modes we will most likely charge the battery quicker than expected.

Constant Charge (CC):

The principal mode to get into activity will be the CC mode. Here the measure of charging current that ought to enter the battery is fixed. To keep up this current the voltage will be shifted likewise.

Constant Voltage (CV):

When the CC mode is finished the CV mode will kick in. Here the Voltage will be kept fixed and the present will be permitted to change according to the charging prerequisite of the battery.

For our situation we have a 7.4V Lithium battery pack, which is only two 18650 cells of 3.7V each is associated in arrangement (3.7V + 3.7V = 7.4V). This battery pack ought to be charged when the voltage reaches down to 6.4V (3.2V per cell) as well as can be charged upto 8.4V (4.2V per cell). Thus these qualities are as of now fixed for our battery pack.

Next we have chosen the charging current in CC mode, this can typically found in the datasheet of the battery and the worth relies upon the Ah rating of the battery. For our situation I have chosen an estimation of 800mA as Constant Charging current. So at first when the battery is associated for charging the charger ought to get into CC mode and push in 800mA into the battery by differing the charging voltage concurring. This will charge the battery and the battery voltage will begin to increment gradually.

Since we are pushing an overwhelming current into the battery with higher voltage esteems we can't leave it in CC till the battery gets completely energized. We need to move the charger from CC mode to CV mode when the battery voltage has arrived at an extensive worth. Our battery pack here ought to be 8.4V when completely energized so we can move it from CC mode to CV mode at 8.2V.

When the charger has moved to CV mode we ought to keep up a consistent voltage, the estimation of steady voltage is 8.6V for our situation. The battery will deplete an extensively less present in CV mode than CC mode from the battery is nearly charged in CC mode itself. Consequently at a fixed 8.6V the battery will expend less present and this present will go diminish as the battery gets charged. So we need to screen the present when it arrives at an exceptionally low worth state under 50mA we accept that the battery is completely energized and separate the battery from the charger consequently utilizing a transfer.

To summarize we can list the battery charging procedure as follows

1. Enter CC mode as well as accuse the battery of a fixed 800mA Regulated current.

2. Screen the battery voltage and when it arrives at 8.2V move to CV Mode.

3. In CV mode accuse the battery of a fixed 8.6V Regulated Voltage.

4. Screen the charging present as it gets decreased.

5. At the point when the present arrives at 50mA detach the battery from charger consequently.

The qualities, 800mA, 8.2V and 8.6V are fixed in light of the fact that we have a 7.4V lithium battery pack. You can undoubtedly change these qualities according to the necessity of your battery pack. Additionally note that there exist many stage chargers. A two phase charger like this is the most generally utilized one. In a three phase charger the stages will be CC, CV and buoy. In a four or six phase charger the inner obstruction, temperature and so forth will be considered. Presently, that we have a short comprehension of how the Two stage charger ought to really work, how about we get into the Circuit Diagram.

Circuit Diagram

The total circuit chart for this lithium battery charger can be found underneath. The circuit was made utilizing EasyEDA and the PCB will likewise be manufactured utilizing the equivalent.

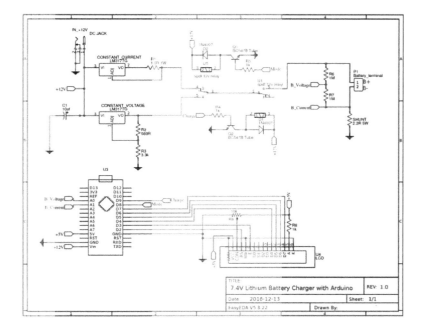

As should be obvious the circuit is quite straightforward. We have utilized two LM317 Variable voltage controller ICs, one to manage Current and the other to direct Voltage. The principal transfer is utilized to switch among CC and CV mode and the subsequent hand-off is utilized to associate or disengage the battery to the charger. How about we break the circuit into fragments and comprehend its structure.

LM317 Current Regulator

The LM317 IC can go about as a present controller

with the assistance of a solitary resistor. The circuit for the equivalent is demonstrated as follows

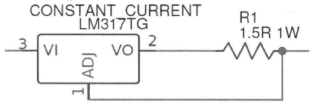

For our charger we have to direct a current of 800mA as talked about above. The equation for ascertaining the estimation of resistor for the required current is given in datasheet as

Resistor (Ohms) = 1.25 / Current (Amps)

For our situation the estimation of current is 0.8A and for that we get an estimation of 1.56 Ohms as the resistor esteem. Be that as it may, the nearest esteem we could utilize is 1.5 Ohms which is referenced in the circuit chart above.

LM317 Voltage Regulator

For the CV method of lithium battey charger we need to manage the voltage to 8.6V as examined before. Again LM317 can do this with the assistance of only two resistors. The circuit for the equivalent is demonstrated as follows.

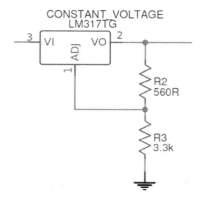

The recipe to compute the yield voltage for a LM317 Regulator is give as

$$Vout = 1.25x(1 + \frac{R2}{R1})$$

For our situation the yield voltage (Vout) ought to be 8.6V, and the estimation of R1 (here R2) ought to be under 1000 ohms so I have chosen an estimation of 560 Ohms. With this in the event that we compute the estimation of R2 we persuade it to be 3.3k Ohms. You can utilize any estimations of resistor mix gave you get the yield voltage to be 8.6V. You can utilize this online LM317 Calculator to make your work simpler.

Relay Arrangement to toggle between CC and CV mode

We have two 12V Relay, every one of which are driven by Arduino through BC547 NPN transistor. Both the

Relay course of action is demonstrated as follows

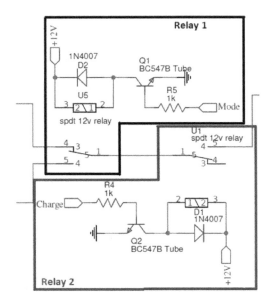

The First Relay is utilized to flip between the CC and CV method of the charger, this Relay is activated by the Arduino stick named as "Mode". Naturally the transfer is in CC mode when it is activated it changes from CC mode to CV mode.

Also the subsequent Relay is utilized to interface or separate the charger from the Battery; this Relay is activated by the Arduino stick named as "Charge". Of course the hand-off detaches the battery from the charger, when activated it associates the charger to the battery. Aside from this the two diodes D1 as well as D2 are utilized for shielding the circuit from turn around current and the 1K Resistors R4 and R5 are utilized to restrict the present moving through the bottom of the transistor.

Measuring Lithium Battery Voltage

To screen the charging procedure we need to gauge the battery voltage, at exactly that point we can move the charger from CC mode to CV mode when the battery voltage arrives at 8.2V as examined. The most widely recognized method used to gauge voltage with Microcontrollers like Arduino is by utilizing a Voltage divider circuit. The one utilized here is demonstrated as follows.

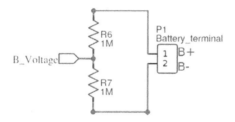

As we probably am aware the greatest voltage the Arduino Analog stick can quantify is 5V, yet our battery could go as high as 8.6V in CV mode we have to venture down this to a lower voltage. This is actually done by the Voltage divider circuit. You can compute the estimation of Resistor and find out about voltage divider by utilizing this online voltage divider adding machine. Here we have concluded the yield voltage by half of the first input voltage, this yield voltage is then sent to the Arduino Analog stick however the "B_Voltage" mark. We can later recover the first esteem while programming the Arduino.

Measuring Charging Current

Another essential parameter to be estimated is the charging current. During the CV mode the battery will be disengaged to the charger when the charging current goes beneath 50mA showing charge consummation. There are numerous strategies to gauge current, the most generally utilized strategy is by utilizing a shunt resistor. The circuit for the equivalent is demonstrated as follows

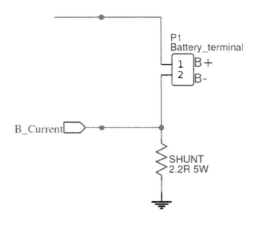

The idea driving it is straightforward ohms law. The whole current streaming to the battery is made to course through the shunt resistor 2.2R. At that point by Ohms law (V=IR) we realize that the voltage drop

over this resistor will be corresponding to current coursing through it. Since we know the estimation of resistor and Voltage crosswise over it tends to be estimated utilizing Arduino Analog stick the estimation of current can be effectively determined. The estimation of voltage drop over the resistor is sent to Arduino through the name "B_Current". We realize that the most extreme charging current will be 800mA so by utilizing the formulae V=IR and P=I2R we can ascertain the Resistance worth and Power estimation of the Resistor.

Arduino and LCD

At long last on the Arduino side we need to interface a LCD with Arduino to show the charging Process to the client and control the charging by estimating the voltage, current and after that setting off the Relays likewise.

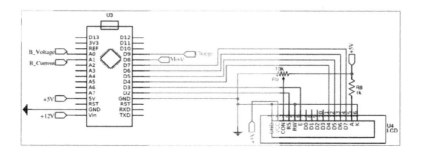

The Arduino Nano has an on-board Voltage controller consequently the supply voltage is given to Vin and the directed 5V is utilized to run the Arduino and

16x2 LCD show. The Voltage as well as Current can be estimated by the Analog pins A0 and A1 individually utilizing the names "B_Voltage" and "B_Current". The Relay can be activated by flipping the GPIO stick D8 and D9 which are associated through the names "Mode" and "Charge". When the schematics are prepared we can continue with PCB manufacture.

PCB Design and Fabrication using EasyEDA

To plan this Lithum battery charger Circuit, we have picked the online EDA instrument called EasyEDA. I have recently utilized EasyEDA ordinarily and thought that it was advantageous to use since it has a decent accumulation of impressions and it is open-source. In the wake of structuring the PCB, we can arrange the PCB tests by their ease . They likewise offer part sourcing administration where they have a huge load of electronic segments and clients can arrange their required segments alongside the PCB request.

While planning your circuits and PCBs, you can likewise make your circuit and PCB structures open with the goal that different clients can duplicate or alter them and can take profit by your work, we have additionally made our entire Circuit and PCB designs open for this circuit.

You can see Layer (Top, Bottom, Topsilk, bottom-silk and so forth) of the PCB by choosing the layer structure the 'Layers' Window. You can likewise see the Lithium battery Charger PCB, how it will take care of manufacture utilizing the Photo View catch in EasyEDA:

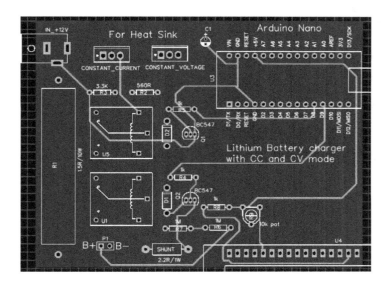

Calculating and Ordering Samples online

Subsequent to finishing the plan of this Lithium battery Charger PCB, you can arrange the PCB through . To arrange the PCB from JLCPCB, you need Gerber File. To download Gerber documents of your PCB simply click the Generate Fabrication File catch on EasyEDA editorial manager page, at that point download the Gerber record from that point or you can tap on Order at JLCPCB as appeared in underneath picture. This will divert you to JLCPCB.com, where you can choose the quantity of PCBs you need to arrange, what number of copper layers you need, the PCB thickness, copper weight, and even the PCB shading, similar to the preview demonstrated as follows:

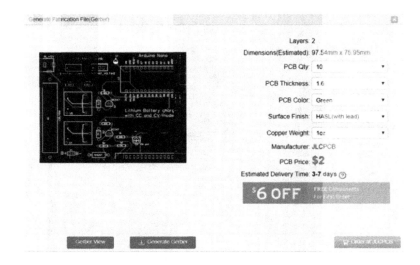

In the wake of tapping on request at JLCPCB catch, it will take you to JLCPCB site where you can arrange the PCB in low rate which is $2. Their fabricate time is likewise less which is 48 hours with DHL conveyance of 3-5 days, fundamentally you will get your PCBs inside seven days of requesting.

Subsequent to requesting the PCB, you can check the Production Progress of your PCB with date as well as time. You check it by going on Account page and snap on "Creation Progress" connect under the PCB like, appeared in beneath picture.

Anbazhagan k

Process		
1MI	○	2018-12-20 10:40:57
2Drilling	○	2018-12-20 11:26:43
3Copper Deposition	○	2018-12-20 13:34:39
4Image the outer layers	○	2018-12-20 14:28:49
5Pattern Plating	○	2018-12-20 16:21:15
6Automatic Optical Inspection(AOI)	○	2018-12-20 19:53:10
7Solder Mask	○	2018-12-20 19:53:26
8Silkscreen	○	2018-12-20 22:48:35
9Hot Air Solder Leveling(HASL)	○	2018-12-21 01:18:35
10Electrical Test	○	2018-12-21 01:33:04
11Profiling V-cut scoring	○	2018-12-21 03:50:04
12Final inspection	○	2018-12-21 05:36:04
13Packaging Delivery	○	2018-12-21 06:06:51

100%

Following couple of long periods of requesting PCB's I got the PCB tests in decent bundling as appeared in beneath pictures.

In the wake of ensuring the tracks and impressions were right. I continued with amassing the PCB, I utilized female headers to put the Arduino Nano and LCD so I can expel them later on the off chance that I need them for different ventures. The totally welded board resembles this beneath

Programming the Arduino for two step Lithium Battery Charging

When the equipment is prepared we can continue with composing the code for the Arduino Nano. The total program for this venture is given at the base of the page, you can transfer it legitimately to your Arduino. Presently, we should break the program into little bits and comprehend what the code really does.

As consistently we start the program by instating the I/O pins. As we probably am aware from our equipment the pins A0 and A2 is utilized to quantify Voltage and current separately and the stick D8 and D9 is utilized the control the Mode transfer and Charge hand-off. The code to characterize the equivalent is demonstrated as follows

```
const int rs = 2, en = 3, d4 = 4, d5 = 5, d6 = 6, d7 = 7; //Mention the pin number for LCD connection

LiquidCrystal lcd(rs, en, d4, d5, d6, d7);

int Charge = 9; //Pin to connect or disconnect the battery to the circuit

int Mode = 8; //Pin to toggle between CC mode and CV mode
```

```
int Voltage_divider = A0; //To measure battery
Voltage

int Shunt_resistor = A1; //To measure charging
current

float Charge_Voltage;

float Charge_current;
```

Inside the arrangement work, we introduce the LCD capacity and show an introduction message on the screen. We additionally characterize the hand-off pins as yield pins. At that point trigger the charge transfer interface the battery to the charger and of course the charger remains in CC mode.

```
void setup() {

  lcd.begin(16, 2); //Initialise 16*2 LCD

  lcd.print("7.4V Li+ charger"); //Intro Message
line 1

  lcd.setCursor(0, 1);

  lcd.print("-Hello_world "); //Intro Message line 2

  lcd.clear();
```

```
pinMode (Charge, OUTPUT);

pinMode (Mode, OUTPUT);

digitalWrite(Charge,HIGH); //Begin Chargig Initially by connecting the battery

digitalWrite(Mode,LOW); //HIGH for CV mode and LOW of CC mode, initally CC mode

delay(1000);

}
```

Next, inside the vast circle work, we start the program by estimating the Battery Voltage and Charging current. The worth 0.0095 and 1.78 is duplicated with Analog incentive to change over 0 to 1024 to genuine voltage and current worth you can utilize a multimeter and a clip meter to quantify the genuine worth and after that figure the multiplier esteem. It is additionally hypothetically compute the multiplier esteems dependent on the resistors we have utilized however it was not as exact as I anticipated that it should be.

```
//Measure voltage and current initially

Charge_Voltage = analogRead(Voltage_divider) *
```

```
0.0092; //Measure Battery Voltage

Charge_current = analogRead(Shunt_resistor) *
1.78; //Measure charging current
```

On the off chance that the Charge Voltage is under 8.2V we go into CC mode and on the off chance that it is higher than 8.2V, at that point we go into CV mode. Every mode has its own while circle. Inside CC mode circle we kept the Mode stick as LOW to remain in CC mode as well as afterward continue observing the voltage as well as current. In case the voltage surpasses the 8.2V edge voltage we break the CC circle utilizing a break articulation. The status of charge voltage is additionally shown on the LCD inside the CC circle.

```
//If the battery voltage is less than 8.2V enter CC
mode

while(Charge_Voltage<8.2) //CC MODE Loop

{

  digitalWrite(Mode,LOW); //Stay in CC mode

//Measure Voltage and Current

  Charge_Voltage = analogRead(Voltage_divider)
```

```
* 0.0095; //Measure Battery Voltage

  Charge_current = analogRead(Shunt_resistor) *
1.78; //Measure charging current

//print detials on LCD

  lcd.print("V ="); lcd.print(Charge_Voltage);

  lcd.setCursor(0, 1);

  lcd.print("In CC mode");

  delay(1000);

  lcd.clear();

//Check if we have to exit CC mode

  if(Charge_Voltage>=8.2) // If yes

  {

    digitalWrite(Mode,HIGH);  //Change  to  CV
mode

    break;

  }
```

```
}
```

A similar method can be pursued for CV mode moreover. In the event that the voltage surpasses 8.2V the charger goes into CV mode by making the Mode stick high. This applies a steady 8.6V over the battery and the charging current is permitted to change dependent on battery necessity. This charging current is then checked and when it comes to underneath 50mA we can end the charging procedure by separating the battery from the charger. To do this we essentially need to mood killer the Charge transfer as show in the code underneath

```
//If the battery voltage is greater than 8.2V enter
CV mode

  while (Charge_Voltage>=8.2) //CV MODE Loop

  {

    digitalWrite(Mode,HIGH); //Stay in CV mode

//Measure Voltage and Current

    Charge_Voltage = analogRead(Voltage_divider)
* 0.0092; //Measure Battery Voltage

    Charge_current = analogRead(Shunt_resistor) *
```

1.78; //Measure charging current

//Display details to user in LCD

```
lcd.print("V="); lcd.print(Charge_Voltage);

lcd.print(" I="); lcd.print(Charge_current);

lcd.setCursor(0, 1);

lcd.print("In CV mode");

delay(1000);

lcd.clear();
```

//Check if the battery is charged by monitoring charging current

```
if(Charge_current<50) //If yes

{

    digitalWrite(Charge,LOW); //Turn off charging

    while(1) //Keep the charger off until restart

    {
```

```
    lcd.setCursor(0, 1);

    lcd.print("Charge Complete.");

    delay(1000);

    lcd.clear();

  }

 }

 }

}
```

Working of 7.4V Two Step Lithium Battery Charger

When the equipment is prepared transfer the code into the Arduino board. At that point associate the battery to the charging terminal of the board. Ensure you associate them in right extremity, turning around the extremity will make genuine harm the battery and the board. In the wake of associating the battery control the charger utilizing a 12V Adapter. Your will be welcomed with an introduction content and the charger will continue to CC mode or CV mode dependent on the status of the battery. On the off chance that the battery is completely released at the hour of charging it will go into CC mode and your LCD will show something like this beneath.

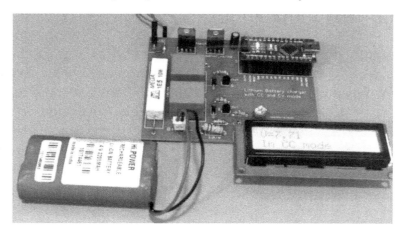

As the battery gets charged the Voltage will increment as appeared. At the point when this voltage arrives at 8.2V the charger will go into CV mode from CC mode as well as now it will show both Voltage as well as current as demonstrated as follows.

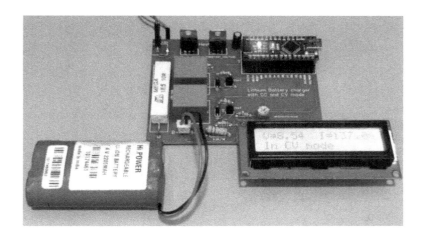

From here gradually the present utilization of the battery will go down as it gets charged. At the point when current ranges to 50mA or less the charger expect the battery to be completely energized and afterward separates the battery from charger utilizing the transfer and shows the accompanying screen. After which you can disengage the battery from the charger and use it in your applications.

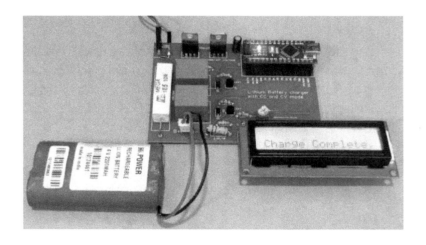

Expectation you comprehended the undertaking and delighted in structure it. Again the circuit is just for instructive reason so use it with duty since lithium batteries are not steady under brutal conditions.

Code

/*

* 7.4V Lithium Two step Charger Code

```
*/
#include <LiquidCrystal.h> //Librarey to use 16*2 LCD display
const int rs = 2, en = 3, d4 = 4, d5 = 5, d6 = 6, d7 = 7; //Mention the pin number for LCD connection
LiquidCrystal lcd(rs, en, d4, d5, d6, d7);
int Charge = 9; //Pin to connect or disconnect the battery to the circuit
int Mode = 8; //Pin to toggle between CC mode and CV mode
int Voltage_divider = A0; //To measure battery Voltage
int Shunt_resistor = A1; //To measure charging current
float Charge_Voltage;
float Charge_current;
void setup() {
 lcd.begin(16, 2); //Initialise 16*2 LCD


 lcd.print("7.4V Li+ charger"); //Intro Message line 1
 lcd.setCursor(0, 1);
 lcd.print("-Hello_world "); //Intro Message line 2
 lcd.clear();
 pinMode (Charge, OUTPUT);
 pinMode (Mode, OUTPUT);
 digitalWrite(Charge,HIGH); //Begin Chargig Initially by connecting the battery
```

```
  digitalWrite(Mode,LOW); //HIGH for CV mode and
LOW of CC mode, initally CC mode
  delay(1000);
}
void loop() {
//Measure voltage and current initially
  Charge_Voltage = analogRead(Voltage_divider) *
0.0092; //Measure Battery Voltage
  Charge_current = analogRead(Shunt_resistor) *
1.78; //Measure charging current
//If the battery voltage is less than 8.2V enter CC
mode
 while(Charge_Voltage<8.2) //CC MODE Loop
 {
  digitalWrite(Mode,LOW); //Stay in CC mode
//Measure Voltage and Current
  Charge_Voltage = analogRead(Voltage_divider) *
0.0095; //Measure Battery Voltage
  Charge_current = analogRead(Shunt_resistor) *
1.78; //Measure charging current
//print detials on LCD
  lcd.print("V="); lcd.print(Charge_Voltage);
  lcd.setCursor(0, 1);
  lcd.print("In CC mode");
  delay(1000);
  lcd.clear();


//Check if we have to exit CC mode
  if(Charge_Voltage>=8.2) // If yes
```

```
  {
   digitalWrite(Mode,HIGH); //Change to CV mode
   break;
  }
 }
//If the battery voltage is greater than 8.2V enter CV
mode
 while (Charge_Voltage>=8.2) //CV MODE Loop
 {
  digitalWrite(Mode,HIGH); //Stay in CV mode
//Measure Voltage and Current
    Charge_Voltage = analogRead(Voltage_divider) *
0.0092; //Measure Battery Voltage
    Charge_current = analogRead(Shunt_resistor) *
1.78; //Measure charging current
//Display details to user in LCD
  lcd.print("V="); lcd.print(Charge_Voltage);
  lcd.print(" I="); lcd.print(Charge_current);
  lcd.setCursor(0, 1);
  lcd.print("In CV mode");
  delay(1000);
  lcd.clear();


//Check if the battery is charged by monitoring char-
ging current
  if(Charge_current<50) //If yes
  {
   digitalWrite(Charge,LOW); //Turn off charging
    while(1) //Keep the charger off until restart
```

```
  {
   lcd.setCursor(0, 1);
   lcd.print("Charge Complete.");
   delay(1000);
   lcd.clear();
  }
 }
 }
}
//**Happy Charging**//
```